REST
Assured

NANCY McGUIRK

REST
Assured

Devotions for Souls
in a Restless World

B&H
PUBLISHING GROUP
Nashville, Tennessee

ISBN: 978-0-8054-4541-1

Published by B&H Publishing Group
Nashville, Tennessee

Author is represented by Alive Communications, Inc., 7680
Goddard Street, Suite 200, Colorado Springs, CO 80920.

Dewey Decimal Classification: 242.5
Subject Heading: DEVOTIONAL LITERATURE \
CHRISTIAN LIFE \ REST

1 2 3 4 5 6 7 8   10 09 08 07

DEDICATION

This book is dedicated with unending gratitude
to my family: my beloved husband, Terry,
and my four precious children,
Meggie, Terry, Missy, and Mary.
You all are the joy of my life.

TABLE OF CONTENTS

TABLE OF CONTENTS

Table of Contents

FOREWORD

When I first met Nancy McGuirk in Atlanta, I knew I had met a kindred spirit. I loved her enthusiasm for God's Word and her tender heart for the women in the Bible class she founded more than seventeen years ago. I also learned of Nancy's passion: ministering to women and the centrality of the Word of God in her teaching. Nancy invited me to speak to the hundreds of women who attend the weekly Women's Community Bible Study. If I lived in Atlanta and wanted to join a Bible study, I would join Nancy's. I have a deep respect for her priorities and values.

Because my own ministry emphasis has been to reach out to those who feel they are not experiencing God's abundant grace, I am delighted to recommend Nancy's new devotional, *Rest Assured*. Within these pages Nancy shares what God has done in her own life: replace striving and struggling with resting in His abundant grace and living in His never-ending resources.

The purpose of this book—to provide rest for souls in a restless world—is extremely relevant today. We do live in a restless world, and we become spiritually and emotionally restless if we do not stay grounded in Christ and His Word. As a busy person myself, I know the most important thing I do each day is spend time with God. This discipline keeps my life centered.

The devotionals in this book are real, applicable, practical, and—best of all—based on scriptural truths. They cover issues we all confront on a daily basis. You will find rest for your spirit, healing for your hurts, and hope for your despair.

After years of walking with Christ, Nancy knows the importance of depending on God's Word daily in her everyday choices. As a busy wife, mother, Bible teacher, and counselor, Nancy's devotionals minister to people of all ages who face the choice every day of living life from God's perspective or the world's. You hold in your hand a wonderful tool to help you learn to depend on God as Nancy has. I highly commend to you the wisdom imparted in *Rest Assured*.

—Ruth Graham

ACKNOWLEDGMENTS

To the members of the Women's Community Bible Study of Atlanta: You are my treasured spiritual family—a gift from God seventeen years ago to teach me about the richness and reality of life in the body of Christ.

To my friends (affectionately called the "Devo Divas"— Marianne Craft, Pam Elting, Hyland Justice, Kathy Lee, and Sheila Shessel) who tirelessly read each devotional, providing feedback, direction, and love: Ladies, you have shown me what it means to live sacrificially for God's glory.

To my editor, William Kruidenier: Your patience, encouragement, and literary advice have been invaluable throughout this process.

To my publisher, Leonard Goss of the B&H Publishing Group: Your enthusiasm, professional expertise, and steadfast support have made this journey a true joy.

To Kim Overcash Stanford, Andrea Irwin, Diana Lawrence, and Mary Beth Shaw of the B&H Publishing Group: Your efforts and excellence in editing, graphics, and marketing have been not only appreciated, but admired.

ACKNOWLEDGMENTS

To my husband, Terry: You were my first, and remain my best, answer to prayer. Thank you for your love and encouragement.

To my children, Meggie, Terry, Missy, and Mary: You remind me each day how incredibly blessed I am. God has taught me most of life's lessons through each of you.

To my Lord and Savior Jesus Christ: Dear Jesus, because of Your grace and forgiveness, I have a new life, live with new hope, embrace a new purpose, and belong to a new family. Your Holy Spirit inspired this book, and Your powerful words calm my heart each day. May all who read these pages experience the same hope and rest that only You can give. Amen.

INTRODUCTION

*F*or many of us in this busy world, falling into bed at night is the highlight of our day. After chasing little ones around or working hard at a job—not to mention tending to the never-ending list of personal to-dos—the bed is a welcome refuge. Crawling into silence, warmth, and security is the perfect way to end a hectic day.

As much as I welcomed going to bed, however, over time I discovered that only part of me was winding down and resting. My body would relax, but my heart and mind were still working at full speed. The more challenging my day had been, the more challenging it was to fall asleep and rest—the kind of rest I knew I needed.

Eventually, as I grew as a Christian, I discovered there are different kinds of rest and that they're connected. There's physical rest, but more importantly there's spiritual (mental and emotional) rest. I began to learn that the more rested I was spiritually, the stronger I was physically. The more I learned to rest in God—let Him be God instead of me playing His role—the more I could stop worrying about things that were beyond my control anyway.

Busy people are always looking for rest—spiritual peace and contentment—but often in all the wrong places. We look for rest on vacations, in recreation, in spending sprees, in changing relationships, in careers, in the accomplishments of our children—all the while not realizing that real rest is found only in God through a relationship with His Son, Jesus Christ.

Saint Augustine said our hearts are restless until they find their rest in God. I imagine Augustine drew his inspiration from Scriptures like Psalm 46:10: "Be still, and know that I am God."

Jesus Christ issued an invitation to "all who are weary and burdened." "Come to me," He said, "and I will give you rest. Take my yoke upon you and learn from me, for I am gentle and humble in heart, and you will find rest for your souls." (Matt. 11:28–29) *Rest for my soul*—that's what I need on a daily basis.

Here's something else Jesus said that appeals to me more than the enticements of this world: "Peace [rest] I leave with you; my peace [rest] I give you. I do not give to you as the world gives. Do not let your hearts be troubled and do not be afraid" (John 14:27).

Spending time meditating on the words of Jesus as recorded in the Bible is a prescription for finding rest. Henry Drummond pointed out that rest is not some holy feeling that comes on us in church but a state of calm arising from a heart deeply and firmly established in God. And the way our minds get rooted and established in God is by renewing them through the reading of His Word (see Rom. 12:2).

Many of us don't know it is actually possible to go from romanticizing about rest to actually resting in today's world. We dream about being at peace in the midst of our hectic lives without realizing that Jesus has invited us to internalize His words and live in His presence and experience the rest that only He provides.

We don't have to carve hours or days out of our schedules to find rest or buy the latest top-of-the-line mattress set. Rather, we only have to enter into a continuous relationship with God through Jesus Christ. If we would but take a few minutes each day to draw near to Him, to meditate on the truths of His Word, we would find ourselves transformed from frantic to faithful, from hurried to hopeful, from panicked to peaceful.

Therein lies the purpose of this little book: to be a tool for you to draw near to God daily and find rest for your soul. When you believe God's Word—"Do not let your hearts be troubled and do not be afraid"—your heart and mind will be renewed. Rest assured you will find a peace that will not leave you regardless of how busy your life or troubling your circumstances.

Yes, I still love to crawl under my comforter at the end of the day. What's different now is that, with the Spirit of Christ as my *full-time* Comforter, I'm at rest before I ever reach the bed. Trusting in the promises of His Word has made the difference for me, as I pray it will for you.

Now we who have believed enter that rest.

HEBREWS 4:3

PRESCRIPTION FOR REST

You will keep in perfect peace him whose mind is steadfast, because he trusts in you.

ISAIAH 26:3

*W*henever I see an advertisement for a sleeping pill, I am reminded of the verse of Scripture that I have come to use as my own prescription for a good night's sleep: Isaiah 26:3. I find that many of my longest and most meaningful conversations with God are at night before falling asleep. As I give Him my concerns, He reminds me of His promises. As I meditate upon His promises, His peace cradles me into a restful sleep: "Father, I am sorry to bother you with my concerns tonight."

Child, give me all your worries and cares for I am always thinking of you and everything that concerns you (see 1 Pet. 5:7).

"Father, I need you. I do not know which way to turn. I am at a total loss. Please guide me during this crisis and give me wisdom."

Beloved, if anyone asks Me for wisdom, I will give it. If you will trust Me, I will direct your path. I am at work to bring good to you in everything you experience. Do you believe Me? (see James 1:5; Prov. 16:9; Rom. 8:28).

"Yes, Lord. But I don't understand why this had to happen. Couldn't you have stopped it?"

Dear one, My ways are not your ways; My ways are higher than your ways. I know the plans I have for you, plans to give you a future and a hope. Trust in Me and lean not on your own understanding (see Isa. 55:8–9; Jer. 29:11; Prov. 3:5–6).

"Yes, Lord. I will trust you. Thank You for hearing my prayer." Even if your pillow is damp from weeping, know that God sees and remembers each of your tears (see Ps. 56:8). He knows your hurt and your heart—not just at night but all day long. He wants you to hear from Him by meditating on His promises. Instead of tossing and turning in your bed at night, turn the pages of Scripture through your mind. Give Him your concerns, listen for His assurance, and let your mind be at peace and your body be at rest.

Heavenly Father,

When I talk to You in the still of the night, may Your Spirit bring to my mind the truths that will bring peace and rest to my soul. Amen.

——————— *For the rest of your life . . .* ———————

exchange your personal unrest for the peace of God.

2

Why We Worry

Do not be anxious about anything,
but in everything, by prayer and petition,
with thanksgiving, present your requests to God.
PHILIPPIANS 4:6

We all know worrying does no good, yet we do it anyway. We explain our worry by saying, "But that's just part of human nature." Part of *fallen* human nature, yes. Our sinful, fallen human nature always demonstrates what being separated from God looks like. It looks like "fear"—fear that we are in this alone, fear of what the future holds, fear that life is spinning out of our control.

As God's beloved children, we are called to faith, not fear. Faith says, "God is in charge of my life"; "I will trust God even when my circumstances would suggest otherwise"; and "I believe God loves me and knows what's best for me." Faith always crowds out fear.

Jesus gives us a clear alternative to worry. He tells us to turn our worries into prayers (see Phil. 4:6). Prayer is simply a way of demonstrating our faith in God (see Heb. 11:6). We pray because we have faith that God hears our prayers (see Matt. 7:8). We pray

8

because we know God has not left us alone (see Heb. 13:5). And we pray because God calls us to pray (see Matt. 7:7).

When you pray with a trusting heart, you will experience what the apostle Paul promised the Philippians: "And the peace of God, which transcends all understanding, will guard your hearts and your minds in Christ Jesus" (Phil. 4:7). Paul was in jail when he wrote those words and probably wondered if his life was about to end, yet he wrote, "Do not be anxious about anything." He even said, "I have learned to be content whatever the circumstances" (4:11). Why? Because he replaced fear with faith and worry with prayer.

The next time you face a concern or fear, and worry begins to plague your heart, do what Paul did: through prayer, put your faith in a God who has everything under control, and watch your panic be overcome by His peace.

Heavenly Father,

Forgive me for the many times I have worried about things in my life. Help me to put my faith in You and Your love and not my circumstances. Amen.

For the rest of your life . . .

turn your worries into prayers and your fears into faith.

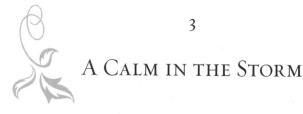

3

A CALM IN THE STORM

He got up and rebuked the wind and the raging waters;
the storm subsided, and all was calm.

LUKE 8:24

*I*n the summer when our children were younger, I often sat on the beach and watched my husband take them out on a small sailboat. He loves to sail and excelled at tipping the boat almost over on its side, making the children scream in mock fear and true delight. As scared as they were, they knew their father was in control. They'd done this so many times before that they knew they were safe with him. So they held on to the boat and one another, screamed as loud as they could, and laughed all the way back to shore. They were calm in the midst of the waves.

Sometimes our lives are like a storm at sea. When we cry out to Jesus, He may calm the storm, but more often He calms us in the midst of the storm.

Mothers live in storms every day. With four teenagers I often find myself rowing and rowing and feeling like I am going nowhere. No sooner have I rowed upstream with one child and feel like I am making progress, than I find myself drifting downstream with another. I need a rudder to keep me headed in the right direction when strong winds blow.

Jesus becomes our rudder as we spend time getting to know Him and listening to Him speak to us. As we know Him better, we understand that He is totally to be trusted with not only our lives but also the lives of our children. If we don't get to know Him, we will listen to the world. Advice from the world is like hidden shoals or sharp boulders beneath the surface, which rip into our lives and cause a flood to come pouring in.

When we are caught in the storms of life, it is easy to think that God has lost control and that we're at the mercy of the winds of fate. In reality, God is sovereign. He controls the boat. As we spend time getting to know Him and experience His love, we learn to trust Him no matter how large the waves and no matter how scary the storm.

Heavenly Father,

I know the waves are coming, and I want to be ready. I'm not asking You to keep me from the storms, but I am asking You to take me through them. Amen.

———————— *For the rest of your life . . .* ————————

you will be safer in the midst of a storm with Jesus than in peaceful waters without Him.

4

BEING BEFORE DOING

*"Martha, Martha," the Lord answered, "you are worried
and upset about many things, but only one thing is
needed. Mary has chosen what is better, and it will not
be taken away from her."*

LUKE 10:41–42

What brings you satisfaction in life? One thing that satisfies me is getting things done—seeing my to-do list get shorter as the day moves forward. The problem with getting things done is having to be in control. But for a Christian, control is something we're asked to yield to the Spirit, to trust God for what does and doesn't get done in a day. Sometimes our actions indicate louder than our words just who we think should be in control.

In the story of Mary and Martha (see Luke 10:38–42), Jesus gives us His perspective on priorities: the difference between doing and being—and which is more important. When visiting two sisters one day, Jesus found Martha bustling around the house, busy with preparations. Mary, on the other hand, sat down at the feet of Jesus to listen to Him, which didn't sit well at all with Martha. Martha's attitude drew a gentle rebuke from Jesus, saying Mary had chosen the best thing: being over doing.

Mary found it is more important to listen to Jesus than to do for Jesus. He was not saying that what Martha was doing was unimportant. Rather, He was saying that if we have not spent time sitting at His feet before focusing on our to-do lists, all our activity amounts to just so much pot banging and dish breaking. Our day can lose its focus, and our activities can lose their purpose without His guiding hand.

When Jesus said only one thing is needed, He wasn't exaggerating. What is needed to move forward in our Christian walk? Sitting at the feet of Jesus, looking into His face, and hearing His words each day. Why is this so hard for us? Like Martha, we would rather be busy, focusing on our abilities and our achievements. But life is not about us. Life is about Jesus and what *He* can do through us. On whom will you focus and put your trust in today?

Heavenly Father,

Please help me to learn that spending time with You is the single most important thing I can get done in my day. Help me to learn the priorities of Your kingdom. Amen.

———— *For the rest of your life . . .* ————

don't confuse religious busyness with spiritual oneness with Jesus.

5

DIGGING YOUR
ROOTS DEEPER

*Every branch that does bear fruit he prunes
so that it will be even more fruitful.*
JOHN 15:2

Several years ago my Lady Bankshire roses that grow up one side of my house looked completely lifeless after a winter storm. I was brokenhearted. But I pruned them and nurtured them through the winter, and, sure enough, they came back the next year more beautiful than ever. It's amazing how storms seem to make plants stronger. Plant breeders, when seedlings are young, will actually brush their hands across the tops of the tiny plants several times a day to simulate the buffeting of a storm; it stimulates root development as the plants anchor themselves against the "wind."

Pruning and storms make us stronger in the Christian life as well. The *New Living Translation*'s version of James 1:2–3 suggests such: "Dear brothers and sisters, whenever trouble comes your way, let it be an opportunity for joy. For when your faith is tested, your endurance has a chance to grow."

Every gardener has more than one set of pruners and cutters; and the sharper they are, the more fruitful the resulting cut. I have noticed that my world is filled with pruners that God uses to make me grow deeper and stronger. Inside the walls of my home live four teenage pruners whom God uses daily to trim me when and where needed. Pruners are at home, at work, at church, in the neighborhood—everywhere we go. And they don't even know how they're being used! In fact, it's not what other people do but my reaction to them that matters. My unspiritual reactions, not their actions, cause the pain of pruning.

So when trouble comes my way, I know it's only going to become major trouble if I let it. And if I do, then I know God will use it to prune and perfect my faith—to cause my roots to grow deeper and deeper into Christ so I'll be ready for the next storm that hits.

Heavenly Father,

Storms and pruning are not my idea of enjoyment. But I know they are necessary for me to grow stronger and more fruitful. I am ready, Lord. I will trust in You. Amen.

For the rest of your life . . .

be willing to be pruned in order to bear much fruit.

6

TAMING THE TONGUE

Keep your tongue from evil and your lips
from speaking lies.
PSALM 34:13

I cringe at the number of times I have spoken without thinking. The power of the tongue is easily forgotten. Proverbs
21:23 says, "He who guards his mouth and his tongue keeps
himself from calamity." And Ecclesiastes 3:7 says there is "a time
to be silent and a time to speak."

Words can have a penetrating effect on one's spirit: "The
tongue has the power of life and death, and those who love it will
eat its fruit" (Prov. 18:21). The greatest disease of the tongue is
gossip: "The words of a gossip are like choice morsels; they go
down to a man's inmost parts" (26:22). It causes more trouble
among the people of God than one could imagine. We deceive
ourselves by thinking that we are lifting ourselves up by putting
others down. And that is just what the enemy would have us
think.

Avoid gossip at all cost. It's a subtle sin that lures the unaware
down its destructive path. We forget that we will be judged by
every careless word that comes out of our mouth (see Matt.
12:36–37). But it's not just the words of our mouths that indict

us. If we listen and receive the gossipy words of another, we are mutually guilty. God sees the heart as well as He hears the tongue.

When the Holy Spirit is at work in us, our words bring life to others. If Jesus' words were both encouraging and edifying, then our words should be as well. That is what I love about the apostle Barnabas (he was known as Son of Encouragement; see Acts 4:36). He always lifted up those around him and built up his brothers in Christ. No wonder Paul took him along on his missionary journeys as a colaborer in the gospel.

James's words are apropos: "Everyone should be quick to listen, slow to speak and slow to become angry" (1:19). May our tongues be instruments of blessing, not destruction; of love, not disdain.

Heavenly Father,

Please forgive me for the times my words have caused hurt instead of blessing. I ask the Holy Spirit to be a check on my speech; to remind me to think before speaking. Amen.

———— *For the rest of your life . . .* ————

govern your tongue by governing your heart.

His Strength in
Your Weakness

"My power is made perfect in weakness."
2 CORINTHIANS 12:9

*I*f you want others to see Christ in you, they need to see your human weakness, not your strength. Our need for Christ, not our self-sufficiency, draws others to Him. God extends His grace generously to those who choose to be humble (James 4:6). But sometimes God allows us to experience humbling circumstances in order to see our need for His grace and power.

The apostle Paul was given a special opportunity to visit "the third heaven" where he heard "inexpressible things" (2 Cor. 12:1–6). To keep him from boasting about this experience, Paul was given a thorn in the flesh to humble him. His request for God to remove the thorn was answered with a provision of grace to endure it. Therefore Paul says he would boast all the more gladly about his weakness "so that Christ's power may rest on me" (12:9). Paul wanted his own strength to decrease so the strength of Christ could increase.

How many times have you experienced a thorn in your own flesh? Maybe your pride took a beating, a friend hurt you, an illness slowed you down, or fear of a future circumstance paralyzed you. Accept that thorn from God. Every time we realize we are not in control, we are reminded who is.

The only way to experience the power of Christ is to come to the end of everything in self. Be careful if you have experienced a spiritual achievement or opportunity from God. It's possible a humbling circumstance could follow. But when life becomes too hard to bear, how sweet it is to fall into the loving arms of the Father's embrace. As we let loose of everything we normally hold on to—reputation, achievement, pride—and cling to God's sufficiency and grace, others will be encouraged to see Him as their resource as well. How wonderful our God is, who keeps us weak enough that we might grow in the sufficiency of Christ and not in our own.

Every time you receive a thorn, remember that roses grow in the midst of thorns. Yet the beauty of the rose captures our attention. The Gardener knows that each thorn is a necessary part of bringing forth beauty.

Heavenly Father,

Remind me that I need to fear my strength more than my weakness. Help me to glory in Christ's strength in the midst of my humbling circumstances. Amen.

————— *For the rest of your life . . .* —————

see your thorns as necessary for revealing the beauty of Christ in you.

19

GUILT: TRUE OR FALSE?

Let us then approach the throne of grace with confidence,
so that we may receive mercy and find grace
to help us in our time of need.

HEBREWS 4:16

One day I met privately to pray with a woman who had struggled with a difficult past. Her father had abused her growing up. She had sought counseling over the years but was still haunted by the abusive words her dad said to her. She could not get free from her sense of unworthiness. Even though she had done nothing wrong, she had been made to feel guilty her whole life, and she could not gain any self-confidence. Her father, after becoming a Christian, admitted that he too felt guilty over the past and what he had done to his daughter.

Only one person had done something wrong, but two people felt guilty for two different reasons—one legitimate and the other not. The father should have felt guilty over what he had done to his daughter. His guilt was true guilt. But the daughter had done nothing wrong and shouldn't have felt guilty, but she did. Her guilt was false guilt. False guilt comes from the devil who is the "father of lies" (John 8:44). She was listening to a voice that was lying to her, telling her she was unworthy and that she deserved to be abused.

True guilt comes from the Holy Spirit (see John 16:8). We are supposed to feel guilty when we sin. Guilt motivates us to repent; it moves us forward. The results of being convicted of true guilt are the fruit of the Spirit (see Gal. 5:22–23), but the results of false guilt are shame, unworthiness, and condemnation.

The Holy Spirit's ministry is to point the sinner to Christ through the conviction of sin. If a Christian is guilty and the Holy Spirit is convicting her, she will be mobilized. But if the guilt is false and the devil is condemning her, she will be paralyzed. If you feel guilty, make sure it's for the right reason and take the appropriate steps: repent if it's true guilt; resist the devil if it's false guilt. And thank God for the blood of Christ that removes the stain of all guilt.

Heavenly Father,

Thank You for sending the Holy Spirit to cleanse me from my true guilt and deliver me from my false guilt. Thank You that I do not have to live with guilt anymore. Amen.

———— *For the rest of your life . . .* ————

let the gift of true guilt move you to confess and make things right with God and others.

9

GROWING THROUGH FAILURE

*The LORD said to Joshua, "Do not be afraid;
do not be discouraged."*
JOSHUA 8:1

hen Jesus met a fisherman named Peter, His first words were, "Come, follow Me." When Jesus later spoke to Peter the apostle, His last words were, "You must follow Me." Between those two commands, and until the end of his life, Peter never stopped following Jesus. But he certainly stumbled.

We may wonder what qualities Jesus saw in a plain, and often impetuous, fisherman that He would choose him to be His disciple. Thankfully for Peter, and for us as well, when God chooses followers, He does not choose on the basis of who we are but who we can become. And that truth implies the possibility, indeed the probability, of failure along the way. God is looking for real people who can be changed by His love. He begins a work of transformation in their lives, conforming them to the image of His own dear Son (see Rom. 8:29).

Knowing that Jesus called, and kept, Peter in spite of his failures gives the rest of us great hope. Knowing that Peter

22

accomplished great things for the kingdom of God lets the rest of us know that God can use us in spite of our shortcomings.

My favorite story about Peter is when he got out of the boat in the middle of the storm and started walking toward Jesus. I love Peter's impulsiveness and his faith. I also identify with the fact that when he took his eyes off Jesus, he began to sink. I don't fault Peter for failing in faith. How many times have I started out strong and ended weak myself? I commend him for reaching out to Jesus when he started to sink and not giving up just because his faith failed him on that, or any other, occasion.

It's easy to get down on ourselves when our faith fails; I don't think anything feels as bad as knowing we've disappointed God. Yet we learn from the experiences of Jesus and the disciples that failure is not permanent. Failure is just a stepping-stone to maturity, a place where God meets us in our day of disappointment and extends a hand. All He asks is that when He says, "Follow Me," we grasp His hand and let Him pull us upward and onward, into the image of His Son.

Heavenly Father,

I have failed You and others so many times. Thank You for not giving up on me. Thank You for calling me to continue following You no matter what I do. Amen.

—————— *For the rest of your life . . .* ——————

live every moment in the reality that God is perfecting us into the image of His Son, Jesus Christ.

HEALING GOD'S WAY

*Though outwardly we are wasting away, yet inwardly
we are being renewed day by day.*
2 CORINTHIANS 4:16

*P*raying with a friend for healing of an illness is a privilege
and a deep responsibility. We have to be prepared for
whatever God's answer turns out to be. While physical healing is our request, we have to agree that God's glory and our
spiritual maturity are greater goals. Regardless of how healing
comes—gradually, suddenly, or not until the person's entrance
into glory—God will answer.

When a friend went through an illness that lasted several
years, not a week passed that I wasn't forced to examine the
difference between talking about faith and living it out. As a
teacher, I taught about faith; but as a sick person, my friend lived
it. Each Wednesday at our Bible study, her friends would wheel
her into the sanctuary where we met. The room would grow
quiet as everyone stared in awe at her joyful countenance. It was
as if the roof opened and a light shone down from heaven and
God said, "This is my daughter in whom I am well pleased."

Though her disease continued to progress, it couldn't
keep pace with her faith. Her family and our community were

touched dramatically by her undiminished faith in God in the face of her illness. She was the manifestation of "not my will, but Thine be done."

My friend came to the Bible study to be ministered to and ended up being the minister. She made all of us realize that we suffer from a disease far worse than her Lou Gherig's disease: the disease of self-reliance. She had become totally God reliant. She put her trust in the One she knew to be trustworthy. Though outwardly wasting away, she was renewed day by day, as were we, through her undying faith.

If something needs healing in your life—body, soul, spirit, or a relationship—know that God's highest priority is your Christ-likeness. Just as Jesus fulfilled His purpose in the midst of great pain and suffering, know that we may be called to do the same. But ultimately, whether in time or eternity, healing will come.

Heavenly Father,

I know there are many areas in my life that need healing: spiritual, emotional, and physical. Bring Your healing in Your time, in Your way. Amen.

———— *For the rest of your life . . .* ————

pursue ultimate health by pursuing wholeness in Christ.

25

The Peace of God

Peace I leave with you; my peace I give you. I do not give to you as the world gives. Do not let your hearts be troubled and do not be afraid.

JOHN 14:27

Two artists were asked to paint a visual representation of peace. After days of toil, they revealed their interpretations. The first artist had painted a beautiful scene of total serenity—majestic mountains, lush grass, the glow of the late afternoon sun reflected on a calm lake in the background. Predictably, the audience was mesmerized by the tranquil setting he had created.

The second artist uncovered his painting and the audience gasped. His painting seemed to be the exact opposite of peace. It was a dark, dangerous scene—explosions, violent winds, people running for safety in a panic. But then a murmur of approval rose from the crowd as they got a better look. In the midst of the horrific scene was a scarred tree with a white dove sitting on a bare limb. In the midst of chaos all around, the bird was asleep, its head tucked under its wing. The first painter had depicted the peace of the world, while the second painter had depicted the peace of God in the midst of the world.

Yes, it's sometimes possible to catch a glimpse of the world at peace—but not very often. The world's peace depends totally on circumstances usually beyond our control. But the peace of God depends only on God's faithfulness and our willingness to receive what He has provided: the security of His promise that the past, present, and future are all in His hands. Through Christ we have the foundation of all peace: peace with God through Christ's reconciling death on the cross (see Rom. 5:1).

But even if we have peace with God, that doesn't mean we'll always have peace with others. Paul said, "If it is possible, as far as it depends on you, live at peace with everyone" (Rom. 12:18). We do what we can to live at peace with others and leave the results to God with whom we know we are at peace. Everyone wants peace on earth and good will toward men, but sometimes it doesn't happen. Even when there is no peace outside, there can always be peace inside because you have peace with God.

Heavenly Father,

Thank You for providing a way to be at peace with You through Jesus Christ. Amen.

—————— *For the rest of your life . . .* ——————

practice the peace of God that passes all understanding
regardless of the circumstances you are in.

27

THE BREVITY OF LIFE

What is your life? You are a mist that appears
for a little while and then vanishes.

JAMES 4:14

Leafing through family photo albums reminds us of at least one thing—how fast the years go by. We see the pictures of our own childhood when we were toddlers holding our mother's hand. Then we see our own children as toddlers holding our hand. And then we see pictures of our children as young adults with their own toddlers. In just a few moments we see the sweep of several generations.

Our journey moves so quickly. We only pass through this life once, and how we use it is totally up to us. C. T. Studd, a famous missionary, wrote this refrain while a student at Cambridge University: "Only one life, 'twill soon be past; only what's done for Christ will last." Life is a glorious opportunity to prepare for eternity. If we miss that opportunity but succeed in everything else, our life will have been a failure. ("What good will it be for a man if he gains the whole world, yet forfeits his soul?" Matt. 16:26.)

You will never live this day again. Are you living it for Christ or for yourself? He wants you to share the gospel with others—

today. He wants you to look for ways to help the less fortunate—today. He wants you to share His love with others—today. When God sees a willing heart, the doors of opportunity are endless.

God wants us to make the most of each day (see Matt. 6:34), yet He has also ordained a time for everything (see Eccles. 3:1). Someone once said that we must work as if everything depends on us and trust as if everything depends on God. Therein lies the secret of using our time wisely: Resting *in* God while working *for* God. See interruptions as opportunities. For all that comes your way has been filtered through the Father's loving hands.

Christ does not want us to live as if this life will continue forever, for it won't. Instead, live life with eternity in view and make everything you do count for the kingdom. And when the pages of your life are turned and it's time to leave this earthly place, may your children remember you as holding the hand of the One who welcomes you home.

Heavenly Father,

Help me remember to live each day as if it were my last. Let me make every moment count for You and Your kingdom. Hold my hand tightly so I don't go astray. Amen.

For the rest of your life . . .

use your time knowing that eternity will reveal how it was spent.

29

13

A HEART
FOR THE HARVEST

*Then he said to his disciples, "The harvest is plentiful
but the workers are few. Ask the lord of the harvest,
therefore, to send out workers into his harvest field."*

MATTHEW 9:37–38

Jesus' mission was to save the least, the last, and the lost. As His followers we are called to do likewise in His name. This calling does not apply just to the missionaries overseas. It applies to every Christian whenever and wherever they are—which obviously means you and me, here and now. The lost are still lost, and the least and last are still insignificant in the eyes of the world. The mission field is all around us: in the workplace, the community, and in your own neighborhoods.

Bob Pierce, the founder of World Vision, prayed, "Let my heart be broken with the things that break the heart of God." Unfortunately, many of our hearts have become cynical toward the plight of the world. We are turned off by financial appeals from charities and missions groups, so we don't do anything. Our hearts need to be broken afresh with the things that break the heart of God.

The apostle James wrote that God has chosen "those who are poor in the eyes of the world to be rich in faith and to inherit the kingdom he promised those who love him" (James 2:5). Maybe telephone solicitors and mail fund-raisers are God's way of giving us the opportunity to get involved. Maybe the homeless person looking for a handout is Jesus' way of saying, "Whatever you did for one of the least of these brothers of mine, you did for me" (Matt. 25:40).

I think Bob Pierce's prayer is appropriate for all followers of Christ. A brokenhearted person will give those in need the benefit of the doubt. Instead of assuming that a needy person will waste or misappropriate what I give him, perhaps I should give and pray that God will use my gift to keep him alive and meet his need while He works in the person's life. Haven't I sometimes misused God's gifts? And doesn't He keep on giving to me?

Ask God to break your heart with those things that break His. Lift up your eyes and look on the fields. When Jesus looked, He had compassion (see Matt. 9:36). May we look and respond the same way.

Heavenly Father,

Give me a missionary's heart. Let me look and see the world with Your eyes. I am willing to go into the fields if You will but show me my place in the harvest. Amen.

For the rest of your life . . .

*avoid breaking the heart of God by learning
what blesses the heart of God.*

14

SEEKING A MIRACLE

Now to him who is able to do immeasurably more than
all we ask or imagine, according to his power
that is at work within us.

EPHESIANS 3:20

any of us have asked God for a genuine miracle in our lives—something beyond coincidence and beyond any human ability. And there have been times when God has answered. But what about the times when, as far as we know, the miracle doesn't happen? The fact is, God does not heal every person or solve every difficulty. Trying circumstances can have a purpose far greater than you or I can understand.

When miracles don't happen, we tend to get frustrated with God—as did some people in Jesus' day. But Jesus resisted those who insisted that He perform miracles, because He knew their real motives (see Matt. 16:4). Their faith in Him was not strong enough without some form of proof. And even if He had worked a miracle, they likely would not have believed. They were seeking miracles to validate their suspicions, not their faith.

Sometimes it takes greater faith to trust God for the outcome if no miracle is forthcoming. The story of Shadrach, Meshach, and Abednego demonstrated this kind of faith. They could have begged for a miracle as they faced the fiery furnace. Instead they told the king, "If we are thrown into the blazing furnace, the God we serve is able to save us from it, and he will rescue us from your hand, O king. But even if he does not, we want you to know, O king, that we will not serve your gods or worship the image of gold you have set up" (Dan. 3:17–18). While they knew God was able to rescue them, they trusted Him completely with their lives regardless of the outcome.

God is at work in every situation according to His purpose and plan, and it is always for our good—whether we see it or not. In everything His goal is to bring us closer to Him. That, in itself, is a miracle. What is more important to you—having a miracle in your life (having life your way) or having the Miracle Worker Himself (having life His way)?

Heavenly Father,

Thank You for working a miracle in my life by causing me to want to love and worship You. Grant me greater faith to ask for and to accept, Your perfect will. Amen.

——— *For the rest of your life . . .* ———

seek first the miracle of an intimate walk with Christ.

15

An Angel of
Encouragement

In humility consider others better than yourselves.
PHILIPPIANS 2:3

A dear friend has been my inspiration when it comes to loving and encouraging others. Every Wednesday morning at our Bible study, she leaves notes of encouragement for hundreds of women in the pews where they sit—a reminder of how much Jesus loves them at that very hour.

But her love goes beyond words on paper. You can't walk by her without getting a hug and a loving, often humorous, word of encouragement. Her self-deprecating manner has endeared her to our Bible study community. She lives to serve Jesus by serving others.

But then our faith community was called on to encourage the encourager. When her husband was diagnosed with a terminal illness, friends from far and wide began streaming to their home to see what they could do to help. The outpouring was so great that it began to sap his strength. To protect his waning health, they had to limit the many visitors to the house.

My friend's husband became her primary "encourager." If love and encouragement alone could heal disease, then he would have been completely cured. He was, of course, in the best of human hands and divine hands as well. The grace of God was plainly evident in my friend's life. As her husband trusted God for his future, she trusted God with the future of her best friend and her family. As our Bible study members ministered to our dear friend, we were ministered to more by watching her keep her eyes on Jesus and His perfect plan for her family.

This saintly encourager is like another Person who, because of His words of hope to others, was followed by crowds who thronged around Him. People loved to be around Jesus, and they love to be around our friend because of Jesus in her. She walked through her time of testing with her feet barely touching the ground, so numerous were the arms of faith lifting her up. We all need angels of encouragement, and we all need to be encouragers as well. May we too have hope and healing in our wings for those who hurt.

Heavenly Father,

Teach me to put others' interests before my own; to be an angel of encouragement in word and deed. Amen.

———— *For the rest of your life . . .* ————

focus on others in the same way
Jesus focuses on you.

35

16

HEARING THE
SILENCE OF GOD

"For my thoughts are not your thoughts,
neither are your ways my ways," declares the LORD.
ISAIAH 55:8

One thing I have learned is that God does not do things the way I would. Every time I expect God to act "my way," I become disappointed with Him. Most often, it is when I pray expecting God to respond a certain way that I get no answer. All I hear is silence.

When it comes to wondering where God is, we are in good company. In biblical days the disciples cried out to God in the upper room in the hours after the crucifixion of their leader, but there was only silence. When Mary and Martha mourned the death of their beloved brother and desperately needed Jesus . . . no response. When Joseph sat at the bottom of a pit having been put there by his brothers to die, where was God? Even when Jesus prayed three times for deliverance and cried out to God at Calvary, "Why have you forsaken me?" . . . nothing.

Looking back at each of these examples, we see that God was very much present and very much responding. In fact,

He was preparing some of His greatest miracles ever. But in this life, God's plan is not always clear at the hour when we pray. In the story of Job, no one experienced the silence of God more, yet God finally made it clear that He owes no explanation. We see dimly through a glass now (see 1 Cor. 13:12), but one day we will see everything clearly. Regardless of how God responds, He may not give His children what they want, but He will give us what we need.

Waiting is a way of hearing the silence of God—a way of hearing what God is trying to teach us. As we depend more on Him, we begin to purge ourselves of what we want and start to focus on what God wants. And often in the deliberate act of not rescuing us or changing our circumstance God performs an even greater miracle and transforms us from the inside out.

When we think God is being silent, the reality is that we may lack ears to hear at the moment. What we perceive as silence today may become loud and clear in the future.

Heavenly Father,

I want to be content with Your ways. When I think You are being silent, help me remember that You are always working in my life. Amen.

—————— For the rest of your life . . . ——————

make a habit of praying for God's ways and will to be done.

37

17

DISCOVERING
WHO YOU ARE

*The Spirit himself testifies with our spirit
that we are God's children.*

ROMANS 8:16

Our family attended a Christian concert where I observed an interesting event while the singer was on stage. I happened to notice a child working her way through the crowd in front of the stage. She made it past the ushers, past security, and ran right up onto the stage. When she ran over to the singer and he scooped her up in his arms, I understood who she was. More importantly, she knew who she was and how her daddy felt about her. And she acted accordingly.

It takes a child's innocence to believe and act confidently. If we're insecure about who we are, it's because we've been listening to the wrong voices. What we believe about ourselves can be compared to the mirrors we look in countless times a day. What is reflected back to us is who we believe we are. Yet all too often, what is reflected back to us is not trustworthy. Without discernment we don't know what to believe and what not to believe.

38

There are two kinds of mirrors by which we decide who we are: God's mirror, which reflects what God thinks of us, and the world's mirror, which reflects the opinions of everyone else. All too often, beginning in childhood, through adolescence (*especially* in adolescence), and on into adulthood, we look in the world's mirror more than God's mirror. That is, we embrace what others are saying or thinking about us more than what God says. The result is a distorted view of who we are. And who we think we are greatly influences how we act.

If your relationship with God is not the equivalent of the singer's daughter squeezing through the crowd, running boldly past the gatekeepers, and jumping into her daddy's arms, maybe you have been looking into the wrong mirror. It's time to read God's Word each day and discover who you *really* are—and act accordingly.

Heavenly Father,

In my mind I know I am Your child. But I want to feel it in my heart and soul as well. Please show me, in as many ways as it takes, that I am Yours. Amen.

—————— *For the rest of your life . . .* ——————

prove you belong to God by approaching Him with confidence.

18

A GODLY HERITAGE

*I have been reminded of your sincere faith, which first
lived in your grandmother Lois and in
your mother Eunice.*

2 TIMOTHY 1:5

Lois was the grandmother of Timothy, the apostle Paul's young protégé, and Eunice was his mother. They were both early converts to Christianity. Timothy's father was a Greek and apparently not a Christian (see Acts 16:1). When the apostle Paul passed through their town of Lystra, he invited Timothy to travel with him. Paul tells us in his last letter, written just before his death, that Timothy's faith was a direct result of the faith of his mother and grandmother.

Timothy was fortunate to live under the spiritual tutelage of two godly women who influenced him for Christ. I believe the faith of a mother or grandmother has a subtle yet lasting affect. Traditionally, mothers spend more time with their children in the maturing years than do fathers. The natural nurturing instincts of women create a profoundly important environment for conveying values and priorities especially the importance of receiving Christ at an early age.

Do your children and grandchildren know Jesus? What are they learning about Him from your life from your verbal as well as nonverbal communications? From the music we listen to, our daily spiritual habits, the books we read, the movies we watch, our ministry to those in need, and the words of grace and kindness we speak . . . every nook and cranny of our lives says something about who we are and children soak it up like little sponges. But there are other, more direct, ways to influence our children for Christ. We can pray for their salvation and spiritual growth (see Phil. 4:6), we can teach them about Jesus (see Eph. 6:4), and we can be an example to them (see Deut. 6:4–9).

While it's good to prepare an inheritance for our children (see 2 Cor. 12:14) and grandchildren (see Prov. 13:22), the most important heritage we can leave them is spiritual truth—faith in Jesus Christ. Proverbs 22:6 says that the best way to ensure future adults will walk with the Lord is to set them on a sound spiritual journey when they are young.

Heavenly Father,

Grant me the grace and wisdom and choices to be everything that I want my children to become; to be a model of what it means to live for Jesus Christ. Amen.

For the rest of your life . . .

wonder not <u>whether</u> you are influencing your children, but <u>toward whom and what.</u>

19

THE CALL TO OBEDIENCE

*Whoever has my commands and obeys them, he is the
one who loves me. He who loves me will be loved by my
Father, and I too will love him and show myself to him.*

JOHN 14:21

If you want to show your love for Christ, there is one way
above all others: obey all that He has commanded you.

There is a reason for every instruction and every command
of God, and they are all for our benefit. But sometimes we don't
feel like being obedient. It's easier to sleep in than to have a quiet
time; we'd rather participate in gossip than have our friends
think we're trying to be "Miss Spiritual"; we justify exaggerations
and flattery by trying to be a "friend" to others. But when we
justify ungodly behavior of any sort, we demonstrate more love
and concern for ourselves than for Christ.

God doesn't use a set of scales to weigh our lives. That is, we
can't expect church attendance, having a quiet time, and giving
money to outweigh disobedience in God's sight. John 14:21 says
that obedience to God's commands is how we demonstrate our
love for Christ. Church attendance, financial giving, devotions,
and other Christian behaviors are pleasing to God, but they don't
cancel out a lack of obedience from the heart.

Motives for obedience are important. Obedience without love and devotion is legalism, and obedience as an end in itself leads to pride. But obedience that stems from a heart of love and gratitude for Jesus is obedience done with freedom and joy and humility. It's contradictory to profess our love for Christ but fail to keep His commands. Jesus Himself asked, "Why do you call me, 'Lord, Lord,' and do not do what I say?" (Luke 6:46).

Are there areas of your life—anger, pride, impatience or others—that you have not given over to Christ in obedience? If we take Christ at His own words, the more we give ourselves over to obedience to His commands, the more of His presence we will know. There are some hard truths about our relationship with God, and this is one of them: obedience matters. When we show ourselves to Him in obedience, Christ shows Himself to us by His presence.

Heavenly Father,

Please help me see the areas of my life that lack obedience to Your commands. I want to know the fullness of Your presence in my life. Amen.

—————— *For the rest of your life . . .* ——————

obey God because you want to,
not because you have to.

20

OUR REFUGE FROM FEAR

When I am afraid, I will trust in you.
PSALM 56:3

We often think that all the great leaders of the Bible were fearless, faithful, and flawless. We see each character as attaining a level of spirituality to which we could never rise. However, some of the people in the Bible we consider strong only got that way after first experiencing times of real weakness and fear.

Moses was afraid to represent God before the Pharaoh of Egypt (see Exod. 4:10). David was afraid to take responsibility for his adultery with Bathsheba (see 2 Sam. 11:15). Eve was afraid not to grasp the opportunity for power that she was offered (see Gen. 3:5). Jonah was afraid to preach to the enemy of Israel (see Jon. 1:3). Hezekiah was afraid to die (see 2 Kings 20:1–3). Peter was afraid to identify with Jesus (see Matt. 26:69–75). Martha was afraid of disappointing Jesus (see Luke 10:40). When it comes to experiencing fear, we're in good company.

What are you afraid of? Rejection from peers? Children hanging out with the wrong crowd? A financial crisis? A life-threatening medical diagnosis? Loneliness? The dangerous world we live in? It's like the preschooler at a pool who tried to decide whether to jump off the high dive. He stood for several minutes on the board ignoring the encouragement of his poolside family. It was not until his father got into the water below the high dive that the little guy made the plunge.

I'm like that little one at times, and I suspect you are, too. Some things we face in life turn us into granite statues—immovable, frozen, unable to take a step. It is not until I remember that God is already in the pool that I am willing to step off into the unknown. The Bible says that God works everything for good for those who love Him (see Rom. 8:28) and that nothing can separate us from His love (see Rom. 8:38–39). So why should I be afraid? Why should you?

Let your fears bring you closer to your Heavenly Father. Instead of being afraid, find your safety in His arms.

Heavenly Father,

Thank You for being everywhere You've called me to be, for never sending me to do anything by myself. Thank You for helping me replace fear with faith. Amen.

For the rest of your life . . .

look at every unknown as an opportunity to see what God will do.

21

THE CURE
FOR LONELINESS

*But I tell you the truth: It is for your good that I am
going away. Unless I go away, the Counselor will not
come to you; but if I go, I will send him to you.*
JOHN 16:7

Mother Teresa once said, "The greatest disease in this world is not AIDS, cancer, or leprosy . . . it's loneliness. It is being unloved, unwanted, and uncared for. . . . There are many who are dying for a piece of bread, there are far more dying for a little love. The poverty of the West is a different kind of poverty." There is a famine in our world not of bread but of love. And the resulting epidemic is loneliness.

A new member of our Bible study shared with me how lonely she had been since moving to our city. She lived alone, had no family close by, had few friends, and was feeling overwhelmed and depressed. Naturally, we rallied some women from the study to reach out and gather her into our midst. During her bout with loneliness we talked about how the ultimate solution to loneliness is the love of God in Christ. It's true that God said it is not good for man to be alone in the long view of things (see Gen. 2:18). And there may be times in all of our lives when we find ourselves physically alone. But that doesn't mean we have to be lonely because Christ is there. To experience His presence we must develop a relationship with Him through prayer and the knowledge of His Word. Every day we walk faithfully with Him is a day loneliness will be overcome in our lives. Jesus is the one who said He will never leave us or forsake us, which means we will never be without the knowledge and experience of His presence (see Heb. 13:5). Because our loneliness has been overcome, we are then able to reach out to others who, not knowing Jesus' presence, are lonely.

The greatest temptations when you are lonely are self-pity and resentment. Remember that Jesus is with you. Regardless of how you feel, *you are not alone.* Stop the spread of loneliness by refusing to give in to self-pity or resentment. And welcome the presence of Christ in your life by being filled with the Holy Spirit.

Heavenly Father,

Please help me remember that Jesus is as close as a prayer, as certain in His presence as a best friend. Thank You that He is always there for me. Amen.

For the rest of your life . . .

be a person who leads others from loneliness to a relationship with Jesus.

47

2 2

THE PERFECT PARENT

Your sons will be like olive shoots around your table.
PSALM 128:3

omeone asked me once if I had ever been on a roller coaster. I said, "Are you kidding? I am a parent of four teenagers."

You may be the parent of one or four or more, but if you're a parent you can identify with the roller-coaster analogy. I know, too, that if you are a parent you are on speaking terms with God. Just as there are no atheists in foxholes, I doubt if there are many in parent-teacher meetings either. The very nature of the task—guiding an immature human being through the trials and tribulations of life (as God does us)—makes us call out to Him consistently.

As soon as we think we have the right to stand up and be praised as the Parent of the Year, we find ourselves flat on our back, dazed by the failure *du jour*. It's not so much that we are terrible parents. It's that God allows new issues to arise that we haven't faced. It's what keeps us depending on Him and learning from Him as He parents us.

Parenting has become an all-consuming task today. Because our culture offers young people so many enticements and opportunities, parents are consumed with trying to respond. So we read books, go to seminars, and talk to our friends—all in an effort just to keep up. And we learn to pray.

I once wrote down all the prayers I could remember that God had ever answered on behalf of my children and how He answered them. It was such a powerful exercise that I keep it in a file so I can refer to it every time I feel overwhelmed. It's God's reminder to me that He is vitally interested in my children's lives.

The biggest mistake we make as parents is thinking our children's lives are all up to us. We forget that they are on loan from God, that He is far more interested in them than we ever could be. Being a perfect parent is not what counts; being a praying parent is.

Heavenly Father,

Thank You for being willing to parent me—and my children through me. Keep me prayerful and careful as I train up those who are rightfully Yours. Amen.

——————— *For the rest of your life . . .* ———————

*observe how God parents you,
then parent your children the same way.*

23

WITNESSING
WITHOUT WORDS

*In the same way, let your light shine before men, that
they may see your good deeds and
praise your Father in heaven.*

MATTHEW 5:16

*M*any Christians worry about friends or loved ones who do not know Jesus. They might go to church and be truly nice people, but there is no evidence of spiritual light or life in their eyes. There is no hunger for God's truth and no conversation about their relationship with God. The saddest part is that they don't realize what they don't have. (Spiritually blind people think their view of life is normal.)

To correct the situation, we take it upon ourselves to tell our unsaved loved ones what we have that they don't. Most of us who have tried this approach know little is gained—except increased frustration for everyone. Yes, talking about the faith is necessary at some point. But until the Holy Spirit awakens in an unsaved person the desire to know about Christ, our talk can fall on deaf ears.

The best way, I believe, to witness for Christ is to be more concerned about our own faith than the lack of it in someone else's life. By spending time in God's presence daily, we will become more like Christ, more yielded and filled with the Spirit. If we follow the Spirit's guidance, He will lead us into opportunities in which Christ's love and light will flow through us to another person who doesn't know Him. We should pray for God to provide a setting and time of His choosing when that person is hungry to hear the truth. Our words might be a seed or may be water on a seed planted earlier. Or we may have the privilege of seeing the harvest as that person embraces Christ.

Someone once said that being an effective witness for Christ means sharing Christ's love in the power of the Spirit and leaving the results to God. Therefore, the best way to prepare to be a witness is by getting to know Christ better and being guided and empowered by Him on a moment-by-moment basis. There is only one Savior, and the more faithful we are to Him, the more clearly others can see Him and come to desire Him for themselves.

Heavenly Father,

Please make me more concerned about the quality of my faith that I might be a sweet aroma of Christ to those who do not know Him. Amen.

For the rest of your life . . .

know that people listen more to who you are than what you say.

51

24

AM I GOOD ENOUGH?

*For it is by grace you have been saved, through faith—
and this not from yourselves, it is the gift of God.*
EPHESIANS 2:8

Our culture places a great emphasis on being the best. I was reminded of this while going through the college application process with two of my children recently. Apparently consultants make a full-time living shepherding high school students through the application maze. How many advanced placement classes did you take? Have you had someone check your essays for content and grammar? How many extracurricular activities have you been involved in? How can we best position you as a leader—a cut above the rest?

It's no wonder that when we begin a relationship with God it's hard to understand—He's not interested in any of the stuff that everyone else thinks is so important. Not that doing our best, being involved, and striving for excellence aren't important to Him; they're just not important in terms of our being accepted by Him. In fact, if the kingdom of God was a college, nobody could get in. "Sorry," God would say, "your grades and qualifications fall too far short. You're simply not good enough for me to let you in."

You can imagine how rebuffed the apostle Paul felt when he was confronted with God's grace on the road to Damascus and in the days following (Acts 9). First, of all, he was *summa cum laude* in the school of rabbinic Judaism (see Phil. 3:4–6), but it didn't matter. Second, he was a persecutor of the church (see 1 Tim. 1:13), and God didn't care about that either. In other words, Paul was neither good enough nor bad enough to affect God's decision about accepting Him in Christ. That's the grace of God.

What matters to God is not how good (or bad) we are, but how "good" Jesus Christ was. All of us have fallen short of God's righteous standards (see Rom. 3:23) and are without hope in this world of being accepted by God. God doesn't choose us "in us," He chooses us "in Christ."

Colleges choose the best—and that's OK. But God doesn't—and thank goodness for that. He extends His grace not because of, but in spite of, who we are.

Heavenly Father,

I'm thankful that You chose me in spite of who I was. As a response to Your grace, help me to become a person pleasing in Your sight. Amen.

--- *For the rest of your life . . .* ---

*extend the same grace to others
that God has extended to you.*

53

Taking Up the Cross

Anyone who does not carry his cross and
follow me cannot be my disciple.

LUKE 14:27

Spiritual exhaustion is natural. When it happens, it affects our attitude and our outlook. Whether you serve in the church or the community, you have probably had the feeling at some point that you've done all you could do: "I've helped in the soup kitchen for years. I deserve a break!" Or "I've led this Bible study long enough. There are plenty of others who should be helping."

I've felt that way too. It's human nature to get tired of serving. We would much rather do our own thing; we'd much rather serve ourselves instead of others.

Whenever I start thinking this way—that I've done too much for Christ—I try to think about what He has done for me. Jesus took up my cross and carried it to Calvary until His broken body couldn't carry it any more and Simon was summoned to help Him.

I'm so glad He never said, "I've been enduring this abuse for several hours now. I don't think I have to go through this any longer. There are others who can take it from here. I've had enough!" Jesus told His disciples that, in order to follow Him, they would have to take up their crosses daily (see Luke 9:23). At the time Jesus told them this, they hadn't seen Him taking up the cross they deserved. But I'll bet they thought about it after seeing Him go to Calvary. They must have; not a single one of the disciples who followed Jesus to the end ever turned back. They all volunteered to serve Him to the end of their own lives.

I pray I won't ever get to the point where I think I've done too much for Christ. If I do, that will be a sure sign that I have begun to devalue what He willingly did for me.

Heavenly Father,

I thank You for what Your Son, Jesus, willingly did for me. Please help me take up my cross and follow Him without holding back. Amen.

—————— For the rest of your life . . . ——————

*take up your cross and follow Christ,
whatever the cost.*

FACTS FIRST,
THEN FEELINGS

It is written: "I believed; therefore I have spoken."
With that same spirit of faith we also
believe and therefore speak.

2 CORINTHIANS 4:13

Martin Luther said, "We must not judge by what we feel or by what we see before us. The Word must be followed and we must firmly hold that these truths are to be believed, not experienced. . . . For the Word must be believed even when we feel and experience what differs entirely from the Word."

One of the greatest temptations in the walk of a Christian is to make decisions based on feelings and not facts. The illustration in the back of Campus Crusade for Christ's *Four Spiritual Laws* booklet has stayed with me since the first time I saw it. A drawing of a train showed Facts as the engine, followed by the next car, Faith, followed by Feelings, the caboose. Feelings always have the least influence in our walk with Christ.

It's true that our feelings are God-given, but they are temporary. When feelings change, the fact of God and His truth remains. God's love is permanent and constant whether we feel

His love or not. We are precious and accepted by God even if others give us reason to feel rejected or unloved. In addition to being temporary, feelings are also fickle. We may feel positive about a challenge or trial one day and negative about the same challenge the next. But the truth is, "With God all things are possible," all of the time (see Matt. 19:26).

What about the fruit of the Spirit—love, joy, peace, patience, kindness, goodness, faithfulness, gentleness, and self-control (see Gal. 5:22–23)? Are these feelings? No, they are the attributes of God lived out through us by the indwelling Spirit of God. They become our characteristics when we are filled with the Spirit. Even though we don't feel happy at a funeral, we have peace knowing that our loved one died in Christ and is with the Lord. The fruit of the Spirit is the evidence of a life based on truth, not feelings.

So line up your three Fs in the proper order: Facts, then Faith, then enjoy the Feelings that come from living a life based on truth.

Heavenly Father,

Forgive me for the times I have lived on the basis of my feelings instead of Your truth. Help me to embrace Your Word as truth for my life. Amen.

For the rest of your life . . .

learn to enjoy feelings,
not depend on them.

57

27

DEPRESSED BUT
NOT DESTROYED

We are hard pressed on every side, but not crushed;
perplexed, but not in despair; persecuted, but not
abandoned; struck down, but not destroyed. We always
carry around in our body the death of Jesus, so that the
life of Jesus may also be revealed in our body.

2 CORINTHIANS 4:8–10

*E*ach of us will face some level of suffering in this life, and we
can expect depression and discouragement to appear when
we think we have no hope. However, trials are not meant to
focus on you but on the sufficiency of Christ in you. Whatever
circumstance or trial you find yourself in, the purpose is so that
"the life of Jesus may also be revealed" in your life.

Corrie ten Boom was a Dutch Christian imprisoned in a
German concentration camp during World War II. Through her
suffering, she vowed to God that if He allowed her to live, she
would go wherever He led her and tell everyone about the love
and forgiveness of Christ. Miraculously she obtained a small
New Testament from a prison worker and began holding Bible
classes by candlelight for a growing group of believers. This

group became known throughout the camp as "the crazy people where they have hope." After ten months of prison and losing her father and sister, Corrie was set free the very week that an order was given to kill the remaining women her age in the camp.

Though Corrie ten Boom could not understand why she had to suffer at the time, looking back she realized that God had used her to give the gift of salvation through Christ to so many before they lost their lives in the camp. Though they endured horrific conditions in prison (and died), they found ultimate freedom and life in Christ. Corrie went on to write nine books and travel all over the world sharing Christ's message of forgiveness and hope in times of trouble. She wanted everyone to know that Jesus is the only place of refuge.

Perhaps you are trapped in an emotional prison right now; you see no way to escape what feels like unbearable pressure. Perhaps your life on this earth is drawing to a close, and fear is setting in. Now is your opportunity to join those "crazy people who have hope" so that "the life of Jesus may also be revealed" in you.

The same Jesus who broke Corrie ten Boom out of a concentration camp can free you from whatever prison you are in.

Heavenly Father,

Forgive me for giving up on You when You never give up on me. Remind me that every trial has its purposes and they all point to Jesus in me. Amen.

For the rest of your life . . .

welcome whatever will reveal the life of Jesus in you most clearly.

28

THE PURPOSE OF PRAYER

*You have made known to me the path of life; you will
fill me with joy in your presence, with eternal
pleasures at your right hand.*

PSALM 16:11

Think about the ways we ask for things and how our motivation changes over the years. When we're little children, we ask our parents for tangible things. At a young age, life is lived in concrete realities: cookies, books, toys, more cookies. When we're teenagers, we move from a concrete world to an abstract one and start asking our parents for advice (though it kills us to do it). As young adults, we ask our parents for something new—not things, or advice, but time: "Could you help me with this . . . ?" Then an amazing thing happens. When we reach adulthood, we begin asking our parents what we can do for them.

All of those requests involve things or activities. But when our parents are in their sunset years, we stop asking about things or activities for them or ourselves. Our focus changes to spending time in one another's presence. We don't even have to talk. Sometimes we can just sit outdoors and enjoy the quiet, or sit by a fire and read books and magazines. Without speaking, we communicate the pleasure of presence.

The pleasure of presence is the purpose of prayer. It takes us varying lengths of time to get to that place, but ultimately we stop seeing God only as a giver of gifts and start enjoying the pleasure of His company. It's fine with God when we do ask—He has invited us to do so: "In everything, by prayer and petition, with thanksgiving, present your requests to God" (Phil. 4:6).

But at some point we recognize, with the psalmist, that "better is one day in [God's presence] than a thousand elsewhere" (Ps. 84:10).

Oswald Chambers wrote, "The point of prayer is not to get answers from God, but to have perfect and complete oneness with Him." And the Danish theologian Sørën Kierkegaard wrote, "Prayer does not change God, but it changes him who prays." Prayer changes us from people who only ask for things, advice, and time, to people who enjoy talking to God just for the pure pleasure of it.

Heavenly Father,

Thank You for hearing and answering my prayers as Your child. I long to learn to enjoy dwelling in Your presence. Help me reach that place of peace and pleasure with You. Amen.

——————— *For the rest of your life . . .* ———————

discover the purpose of prayer by experiencing the pleasure of God's presence.

29

LIVING ABOVE THE CIRCUMSTANCES

So we fix our eyes not on what is seen, but on what is unseen. For what is seen is temporary, but what is unseen is eternal.

2 CORINTHIANS 4:18

Author and Christian educator Howard Hendricks had a favorite reply to someone who said, "Not bad, under the circumstances," when asked how he was doing. Dr. Hendricks would retort, "Well, what in the world are you doing under there?"

From my own experience, there is not a worse place to live than "under the circumstances" whether good or bad. If we live our lives according to our circumstances, we're either pinned to the ground, floating in the clouds, or muddling along in neutral waiting for something to happen. God never intended for circumstances to determine our spiritual frame of mind.

Circumstances can play havoc with our expectations. We expect life to go according to our plans. We plan for a loving spouse, happy children, and a white picket fence—the American dream. But when circumstances go the opposite way, we're done for the day. That's why we should never live based on circumstances because more often than not they do not go the way we expect them to.

When we came to know Jesus personally, we discovered that our lives were not as great as they could have been. We were living up or down, depending on the event of the moment. We discovered that Jesus could come into our lives through His Holy Spirit and make level the way through the peaks and valleys of life. He remained constant and faithful regardless of where the winds of life drove us. Soon, by following Jesus' lead, our lives became more consistent. We learned that the goal of life is not happiness but holiness and that we could be holy (set apart for God's glory) regardless of the circumstances.

God never promised to change our circumstances, but He does promise to change us (see 2 Cor. 5:17). He promises to make us victors instead of victims (see Rev. 3:5; 12:11). So the next time we find ourselves *under* the circumstances, remember Dr. Hendricks's words: "What in the world are you doing under there?" The person we want to be with—Jesus Christ—does not live under any circumstance. And neither should we.

Heavenly Father,

Thank You that every circumstance in life comes to me by Your permission. Teach me to live above every circumstance, seated with Christ in heavenly places. Amen.

———— For the rest of your life . . . ————

refuse to be found under any circumstance, whether good or bad. Only be found with Jesus.

3 0

KNOWING GOD
PERSONALLY

Now this is eternal life: that they may know you, the only true God, and Jesus Christ, whom you have sent.
JOHN 17:3

*E*very Christian knows God but far fewer know Him intimately. I heard someone ask once, "Why do some people seem closer to God than others?" And the answer given was, "Maybe they spend more time with Him."

When my parents met each other, they knew about each other but didn't really know each other that well yet. There was a sense of respect and admiration and a desire to please the other. When they decided to marry, they made a commitment not only to love each other but to be there for each other at all times. This is exactly what happens to us when we accept Christ into our hearts. We have stepped up to the altar and said, "I do."

After over half a century of togetherness, my parents know each other intimately. They know what the other needs without words being spoken; they have always been there for each other. I believe they love each other more today than ever before. They are known by all my friends as the couple that holds hands wherever they go.

Saying "I do" to God means lots of things: I do accept that Your Son died for me to give me eternal life. I do accept that You love me just as I am and are willing to forgive me of my past. I do recognize that You are here for me to turn to and to forgive me of my future sins. I do want a long, loving relationship with You. I want to communicate with You every day, so much so that I know what You want without even asking. I want my love to become totally dependent on You in my life.

Have you been to the altar with Jesus? If you're not sure, it might be time to say, "I do," and then become known as the person who walks hand in hand with God.

Heavenly Father,

I gladly say "I do" to You. I hold out my hand and ask You to take it and allow me to be Your moment-by-moment companion all of my days. Amen.

——————— *For the rest of your life . . .* ———————

find intimacy with God
through devotion to God.

31

YOUR BODY, HIS TEMPLE

For we are the temple of the living God.
2 CORINTHIANS 6:16

We live in a body-conscious world. Everywhere you look there are advertisements for new diet programs or the latest exercise machine. Of course, staying healthy and physically fit is important, it's the foundation for everything else we do.

But there is more than one reason to exercise and eat nutritionally. Some do it to attract others, some do it to look younger, and some do it for health reasons. But all too often our motivations for staying fit are temporary. When a particular goal is met, we lapse back into our bad habits and get comfortable again with those extra pounds. What we need is a permanent reason to stay in shape, one that lasts as long as we live. Fortunately, Christians have such a reason.

The day you became a Christian, another dimension was added to your body: the Spirit of Christ came to dwell in you (see Acts 4:31). Unlike the days of Moses when the Spirit of God dwelt in the tabernacle (see Exod. 40:34) or in Solomon's day when the Spirit of God filled the temple (see 2 Chron. 7:1–3), now the Spirit of Christ dwells in all who believe Him to be Lord.

God wants us to glorify Him in all things, including in our bodies. We are called to present ourselves to God as "living sacrifices" (Rom. 12:1), giving Him complete ownership of who we are. By taking care of ourselves, we are taking care of the place where He dwells. Being lazy and gluttonous is not only unhealthy; it also demonstrates a lack of stewardship of "the temple of the living God." To allow our bodies to fall into disrepair is the New Testament equivalent of allowing the Old Testament tabernacle or temple to begin to crumble. Every Christian is a "living stone." Joined together, we make up the temple of God on this earth today, the place where He dwells (see 1 Pet. 2:5).

If you need a permanent reason to take care of your body through careful eating and regular exercise, let it be to demonstrate your stewardship of part of the creation of God; to provide a respectful place for the Spirit of Christ to dwell.

Heavenly Father,

Forgive me for not always caring properly for my personal part of Your wonderful creation. Renew my will to make choices that glorify You. Amen.

For the rest of your life . . .

let your body reflect the glory of the Lord who dwells within.

32

DIVINE LOVE

*For I am convinced that neither death nor life, neither
angels nor demons, neither the present nor the future,
nor any powers, neither height nor depth, nor anything
else in all creation, will be able to separate us from the
love of God that is in Christ Jesus our Lord.*

ROMANS 8:38–39

*H*uman love" is fickle. Our love for another person can ebb
and flow like the tide; we're close one minute, distant
the next. How people look or how their personality strikes us
can determine the quality of the love we show. How we feel on
a given day can change the quality of our love. Good day, good
love; bad day, bad love. So many variables determine the quality
and quantity of our love.

Not so with God. His love is different: no boundaries, no
variables, no ebb and flow. He loves us in spite of who we are,
not because of who we are. The love of God springs from within
Him and is not determined by what He finds within us. He
doesn't love us because of *our* goodness, kindness, and faithfulness. He loves us because of *His* goodness, kindness, and
faithfulness. He loves because He *is* love.

We are loved by God because of His choice to love. His love flows from Him to us even when we feel unlovable and unlovely; even when we can't receive His love, He is giving it. Our experience of receiving love from God is the same as our giving love to other people. It is too often based on feelings and subject to change. The fact is, nothing can separate us from God's love—not even our feelings of unworthiness (see Rom. 8:35–39). When we remain focused on the fact of His love, we won't be misguided by the presence or absence of feelings. Receiving His love is an act of faith, of certainty, on our part.

Whatever others may do to us that is unloving—abandon us, ignore us, hurt us, reject us, divorce us, speak ill of us—these circumstances have nothing to do with God's love for us. When you feel unloved, remember that nothing can separate you from the love of God in Christ. Regardless of how things may deteriorate around you, God's love remains firm and unchanging. His love is the divine constant in a world of human change.

Heavenly Father,

Thank You that my experience of Your love is unconditional. Please enable me to love others the way You love me. Amen.

——— *For the rest of your life . . .* ———

receive God's love not because of who you are
but in spite of who you are.

69

33

SETTING PRIORITIES

But seek first his kingdom and his righteousness,
and all these things will be given to you as well.
MATTHEW 6:33

Deciding what you're going to do in the next hour is easy—so is the next day, week, even month. Our lives have enough commitments and responsibilities built into them that we can run on autopilot without stopping to think deeply about what we are doing and where we are going. Our decisions tend to be reactive instead of proactive. Sometimes we don't even like to think beyond the immediate future because it scares us. We know that decisions lead to actions and actions reflect our priorities. And if we're not sure what our priorities in life are, then we feel insecure about the decisions we make.

It's easy in our American culture to live an entire lifetime without establishing priorities. If we want it to, our culture will set our priorities for us. We can stay completely busy with careers, shepherding children all the way through college, trying to keep our marriage together . . . and then we wake up one day and wonder if that's all there is. Maybe we grow lonely, maybe we lose our parents, or maybe we experience a crisis of health or finance. Something makes us look at this thing called life, and we ask, "Is this a life I have chosen or one that has chosen me?"

Some who ask that question decide to throw off everything they think has been issued to them—responsibilities, morals, traditions—and strike out to rewrite the script of their future. Others who ask the question come to the realization that establishing the highest priority is the key to ordering the rest. Putting God in His rightful place has a way of making things we thought were cell doors become open doors to freedom and fulfillment. When God is at the throne of our lives, all other things fall in their proper place. Make God your highest priority as you seek Him each day, and the decisions will take care of themselves.

Heavenly Father,

I want You to be my top priority. I want to get directions and marching orders from You each morning. Help me to live proactively, not reactively. Amen.

For the rest of your life . . .

*focus on the priorities of your heart
so your life will mirror those same priorities.*

71

34

BLESSINGS OF BROKENNESS

*Consider it pure joy, my brothers, whenever you face
trials of many kinds, because you know that the testing
of your faith develops perseverance. Perseverance must
finish its work so that you may be mature and
complete, not lacking anything.*

JAMES 1:2–4

The disciples of Jesus experienced a rude awakening after
Jesus' resurrection. They thought He was "going to restore
the kingdom to Israel"—that all their previous troubles were over
(Acts 1:6). If they had only known. The apostle Paul expressed
what they all later learned: "We must go through many hard-
ships to enter the kingdom of God" (Acts 14:22). The path of
discipleship—becoming like Jesus—takes us through everything
He went through, including suffering.

Many new Christians are shocked to discover that becoming
a follower of Jesus doesn't deliver them from all of life's adversity.
The promise to Christians is not that we'll be delivered *from*
adversity but *in* adversity. That is why James encourages us to
count our trials as a source of joy when (not if) we experience
them. The blessing in the midst of brokenness is that we become
conformed to the image of Christ—God's ultimate purpose

for us (see Rom. 8:29). God knows that to be like His Son we must suffer and be broken in this world just as Jesus was. "Although [Jesus] was a son, he learned obedience from what he suffered" (Heb. 5:8)—and so must we. Being like Christ does not come naturally to any of us. Only through difficult situations, when the Holy Spirit gives us power and the desire to make Christlike choices, do we become like Him. That is the blessing of brokenness.

Sometimes God takes away what we have trusted in (peace, security, abundance) in order to teach us to trust Him. We discover that nothing is as dependable and trustworthy as He. After going through enough trials, we begin to learn that He is faithful and will not be moved. By clinging to Him, we will not be moved either.

Brokenness builds our character. We become wiser, stronger, deeper, less impulsive, more stable—in other words, more like Jesus. If you will remember that God's grace is sufficient (see 2 Cor. 12:9), you, like those who followed Him while He was on this earth, will not fear your trials knowing that each one brings you closer to Christ.

Heavenly Father,

Please open my eyes to see the blessings You have for me during my times of brokenness. Help me to draw closer to Christ. Amen.

———— For the rest of your life . . . ————

become whole in Christ
by being broken in self.

73

35

A MARRIAGE
MADE IN HEAVEN

Nobody should seek his own good,
but the good of others.
1 CORINTHIANS 10:24

A friend once told me privately, "My husband is not meeting all my needs." I said, "I hate to tell you this, but . . . he never will." The only person who can meet all of anyone's needs is Jesus. In fact, the only way to make a marriage what God intended for it to be is to have Christ at the center. That means both partners submit to His authority and seek His guidance in every area of their lives.

All marriage partners, at one time or another, have tried to change and control their spouse. But the road to transformation is just the opposite. It is to lay down all sense of power in and of yourself and rely on God's power to transform both you and your spouse. This power comes as the result of the prayers of a godly wife or husband whose main desire is to please God (see 1 Pet. 3:1–7). Godly marriage partners want to *do* right more than they want to *be* right.

As I have grown in my own relationship with Christ, I have also grown in my appreciation for my husband. I have come to see how we complement each other and how God uses him to teach me things that come more natural to him. I know I can't meet all my husband's needs, nor should he meet all of mine (though he comes pretty close). No one can be everything to another person. If we look to Jesus to meet our needs, we will not put unrealistic expectations on each other.

When we pray and ask God to change our spouse, God often shows us that we are the ones who needs changing. To accept your spouse unconditionally (except in abusive situations) and to pray for every area of his or her life, is the way to have God meet both of your needs. Because that is God's design, that's His formula for a marriage made in heaven.

Heavenly Father,

Thank You for supplying all my needs through Christ and thank You for my sweet mate. May we grow together in the knowledge and love of You. Amen.

For the rest of your life . . .

let your disappointment in human relationships cause you to see God's faithfulness more clearly.

36

A CHILDLIKE FAITH

"Let the little children come to me, and do not hinder them, for the kingdom of God belongs to such as these."

MARK 10:14

hy is it we adults have to lose the innocence of youth? Why do we lose our trust in others and create a wall of self-protection that often keeps us living within the prisons of our own minds? When we become children of God, Jesus instructs us to return to the innocence of our youth. He wants us to trust Him with total abandonment and joy, free from the worries and concerns that can so easily dominate our lives (especially since most of what we worry about are things we cannot change). Being free from concerns is not the same as abandoning responsibilities. It is learning to tell the difference so we can give our concerns to the Lord.

When we were young, we jumped out of the bed each day with excitement, anticipating what each day would bring. We did not worry about food, clothing, or shelter. We felt secure, protected, and loved by our parents, and nothing gave us reason for concern.

If we, as adults, would go to Jesus with this type of childlike faith, we would experience that same sense of joy and freedom.

But over the years many of us have been hurt by others. This hurt has affected our trust in people and ultimately our trust in God. We feel the need to take control of life for our own protection. If others are not trustworthy, maybe God isn't either.

But God's love is totally dependable. He wants us to trust Him not just with our fears but with every area of our lives. God in Christ will provide all that we need. He will protect us from evil and guide us each day as we turn to Him. He simply wants us to have childlike faith and to know confidently that He loves us through every circumstance and every trial.

Do you want to understand how to live above the worries of this life? God reveals His truth not to the "wise and learned" but to "little children" (Luke 10:21). Trust in Your heavenly Father. You will rediscover the amazing joy of being absolutely free from concern. You may even regain the joy of your youth.

Heavenly Father,

Help me grow up before I grow old. Help me to become more trusting, more innocent, more willing to follow, more ready to express joy. Help me to lean on You with childlike faith. Amen.

———— *For the rest of your life . . .* ————

look at growing up as more of a spiritual and emotional process than a chronological one.

37

THE BATTLE
OF THE MIND

Take captive every thought to make it obedient to Christ.
2 CORINTHIANS 10:5

*I*dolatry is alive and well in the twenty-first century just as it was in the days of the Old Testament. In those days certain hilltops or platforms in Canaan were called "high places" where pagan worshippers set up sacrificial altars to worship their gods. When Israel entered the promised land, God told the people to demolish all the high places—that is, to cleanse the land from idolatry (see Num. 33:52). Because Israel failed to obey God fully in this matter, she began to worship idols on the high places.

Today many believers are like the Israelites of old. They have affection for God but have failed to cleanse their lives of idolatry. They worship friends, power, appearance, and possessions because they value them more highly than they value God. Just as in the Old Testament, followers of Christ are told to tear down the high places: "casting down . . . every high thing that exalts itself against the knowledge of God" (2 Cor. 10:5 NKJV).

We tear down high places by first recognizing what they are. What consumes your mind more than God? Are you driven to worry or to think obsessively over something that you know is not God's will? What are you striving to accomplish in your life? Who are you driven to please? What are you accumulating? Who or what are you serving with the resources of your life? The answer to these questions will define your high places.

Second, we need to view the mind as a battlefield. If we listen to and become captive to the thoughts of this world, we will live accordingly. But if we listen to and become captive to the thoughts of God, we live as God would have us live. Paul wrote that we are to focus on things that are true, noble, just, pure, lovely, and of good repute; on virtuous and praiseworthy things (see Phil. 4:8). In doing so we will renew our minds and be transformed (see Rom. 12:2).

Because our minds are continually being fed, we are always either putting up or tearing down high places. The only way to be certain we are tearing them down is to defend the battlefield of our mind with the Word of God.

Heavenly Father,

From when I rise to when I retire, may I consciously meditate upon Your Word. Lift up Yourself in my heart! Be the highest place in my life. Amen.

For the rest of your life . . .

guard your mind for what it is,
the gateway to the heart and soul.

79

38

LOSING YOUR LIFE

*For whoever wants to save his life will lose it,
but whoever loses his life for me will find it.*
MATTHEW 16:25

The kingdom of God is a kingdom of paradoxes, a place where we somehow go the opposite direction to get where we want to go, and it works! In the world we grasp to get, we strive to live, and we try to reap without sowing. But in the kingdom we give to receive, die to live, and sow before reaping. Kingdom principles even sound odd to Christians because we're so used to the world's way of living.

God says that we only reap what we sow, so in order to receive we must give. That seems odd to the world, but it's business as usual in God's economy. Here's another: we must die in order to live. Jesus said we're like seeds. We must ultimately die and be planted in the ground in order to spring forth into new life and bear fruit for eternity.

That last paradox has to do with receiving eternal life, but here's a paradox about how to live life right now: you have to lose your life in order to find it. To see how contrary this is to the world's way of thinking, look around—people are doing everything they can think of to find themselves. They're changing careers, changing marriage partners, changing their appearance, changing their medications, changing friends . . . houses . . . cars . . . wardrobes . . . religions. We're a culture in search of itself.

So what does it mean to find your life by losing your life? It means to recognize that we were created by and for Jesus Christ (see Col. 1:16). The moment we embrace that truth, we find the secret to life—we lose our attempts at life (for self) and gain true life (in Christ) instead. We give up more of us in order to find more of Him. As Saint Augustine said, "Our hearts are restless, O God, until they find their rest in Thee." If your heart is restless, go the opposite way of the world and end your search in the arms of Jesus. Then you'll finally be headed in the right direction.

Heavenly Father,

Today I purpose to end the search for myself. Instead, I will invest myself in drawing closer to Jesus, knowing I will find my life as I experience His. Please guide me in that path. Amen.

--- *For the rest of your life . . .* ---

find yourself by first finding Christ.

39

THE SERVICE
OF THE SAINTLY

[Anna] never left the temple but worshiped night
and day, fasting and praying.
LUKE 2:37

Many years ago a woman who sewed clothing for a living also took care of a little boy each day. As she sewed, she shared her faith with this small boy, sowing seeds by her words and deeds that she prayed would bear fruit one day. The actions of this humble woman did indeed bear fruit, for the young boy she looked after was Billy Sunday, who grew up to become one of America's greatest revival preachers.

In 1924 Sunday preached in Charlotte, North Carolina, and a committee of Christian businessmen was formed to continue evangelizing after his crusade. Ten years later that committee brought evangelist Mordecai Ham to Charlotte for another crusade. Among those giving their hearts to Christ at that meeting was a young man named Billy Graham, and the rest is history. The woman who earned a humble living by sewing others' clothes and caring for a young boy didn't do so because she anticipated any direct or indirect results from her efforts. She did it to be faithful and take advantage of whatever opportunity God put before her.

That is a better definition of saintly living than what we sometimes hear. Often "the saints" are those who live humbly and sacrificially, whose good deeds are known by many or have sponsored large acts of charity. In reality, however, saintly service is far more akin to what is done behind the scenes than in front of them.

Jesus set the ultimate example for saintly service when He wrapped a towel around His waist, took a bowl of water, and washed the disciples' feet (see John 13:1–5). This was the job of a servant, not a savior, the disciples thought. They had forgotten that this Savior came not to be served but to serve (see Mark 10:45). Jesus concluded by telling the disciples that just as He had served them, they were to serve one another.

There are an infinite number of ways to fulfill Jesus' instructions to serve one another. But underlying all our service must be the reality that motivated Jesus, a heart of love. Service motivated by love for others instead of love for self is the chief characteristic of saintly service. It's not important that the world sees our service when we know that God does.

Heavenly Father,

I want to be faithful in the moment. Not because of what might come from it, but because it is the right thing for me to do—for a servant to be faithful to the Master. Grant me the grace of faithfulness. Amen.

For the rest of your life . . .

*prove yourself a saint by how you live,
not how long you live.*

40

MAKING DECISIONS

Many are the plans in a man's heart,
but it is the LORD's purpose that prevails.
PROVERBS 19:21

*C*an you imagine the decisions some people face? To commit the nation to war . . . to honor a loved one's living will . . . to be a whistle blower even though it might mean losing your job?

Any decision can seem like a monumental, mind-numbing one if we are not focused on the Lord. There are times when we try to predict what the future will hold if we choose option A or if we choose B. That strategy is a stress producer for sure. Wouldn't it be a relief if we could be assured that whatever decisions we make, God can use them to accomplish His purposes in our lives?

According to Romans 8:28, God has given us such a promise. If we are lovers of God and have entrusted ourselves to His temporal and eternal care, even an unwise decision can be redeemed. Why? Because to those who love Him, He promises to cause all decisions to work for good.

God's primary purpose for our life is to make us holy, not to ensure that we're happy (see Rom. 8:29). In order to achieve that long-range goal, He takes the results of our freewill choices and molds them into forces that will make us holy. If that requires him nicking a corner off here and sanding down a rough spot there on our work-in-progress lives, then that's what He does. He wants us to learn to rely on Him, so self-reliance and self-sufficiency are some of the first things we must give up. While we agonize over our choices, God is strategizing over our character.

Let's remember we are not alone when we make decisions. Our decisions may not be perfect in our sight, but God is perfectly able to use the results of our choices "to will and to act according to his good purpose" (Phil. 2:13)—and our Christlikeness.

Heavenly Father,

Thank You that You can use every decision I make to accomplish Your purposes in my life. Give me wisdom to choose well and faith to trust You with the outcome. Amen.

--- *For the rest of your life . . .* ---

don't limit God's ability to work through your decisions by failing to make them.

41

FAITH THAT ACTS

His faith was made complete by what he did.
JAMES 2:22

When Peter learned that Jesus was going to be killed, he boldly proclaimed, "Even if all fall away on account of you, I never will. . . . Even if I have to die with you, I will never disown you" (Matt. 26:33, 35). You know what happened—just a short time after making those bold statements, Peter denied three times that he even knew Jesus.

It's easy to be critical of Peter for what he did. But, in all honesty, aren't there times in our lives when we would prefer not to be associated with Jesus or with other Christians? Aren't there times when we just wish we could shrink back into a cocoon and not have any expectations placed on us because of our testimony for Christ? We have the record of Peter's bold failure on the night of Christ's arrest in order to show us how vulnerable we are; how easy it is to disconnect our professions of faith from our manifestations of faith. God wants us to have faith that walks, not just faith that talks.

After the resurrection Peter and some of the other disciples had gone fishing, completely confused about what had happened to Jesus. Suddenly Jesus appeared to them on the shore, and they joined Him for a meal. After the meal Jesus asked Peter three times, "Do you love me?" The first two times, Jesus asked, "Do you truly love me, sacrificially?" The third time He asked, "Do you love me as a friend?" Each time Peter answered, "I love you as a friend." He was perhaps still too ashamed of his denying Jesus to profess that he loved Him sacrificially. But Peter did know that Jesus still loved him since He had come to him on the shore. The crux of their meeting was Jesus telling Peter to feed His sheep and follow Him (see John 21:15–19). Jesus wanted Peter to act on the love he professed.

If Jesus asked you, "Do you truly love Me, sacrificially?" what would you say? Professions of faith are good, but manifestations of faith are even better. Let your faith be a faith that acts.

Heavenly Father,

Forgive me for the times I have been embarrassed or ashamed to be identified with You. I don't want to be a coward, Lord; I want to have spiritual courage. Grant it, please. Amen.

———— *For the rest of your life . . .* ————

*always follow your professions of faith
with expressions of faith.*

42

THE PURPOSE
OF A FRUITFUL LIFE

*I . . . appointed you to go and bear
fruit—fruit that will last.*
JOHN 15:16

When we live in dependence on God, the Holy Spirit produces two realities in our life, spiritual fruit and spiritual gifts. Spiritual fruit is what comes to characterize us as Christians (making us like Jesus), and spiritual gifts are the abilities God gives us to build up others in the body of Christ. Each Christian can manifest all the fruit of the Spirit (the character of Jesus) and one or more of the abilities of Jesus (the works He would do if He were still on earth).

Spiritual fruit, especially love, governs the use of spiritual gifts. We can preach, prophesy, know everything, abound in faith, give everything away to the poor, and sacrifice ourselves as a martyr; but if we don't have love, it's all meaningless (see 1 Cor. 13:1–3). The purpose of a fruitful life is to create a setting in which our spiritual gifts can have a meaningful impact on someone else's life. As someone has wisely said, people don't care how much we know until they know how much we care.

In the garden the purpose of fruit is consumption and nutrition. If it is not consumed, fruit rots and becomes worthless. In the spiritual realm the same thing is true. God saved us and gave us His Spirit in order that we might walk in the good works He prepared for us (see Eph. 2:10). God wants our fruit and our gifts to be "consumed" by others so they will glorify our Father in heaven for the change that comes about in their life (see Matt. 5:16).

The way we remain fruitful is to remain in Christ, to abide in Him (see John 15:5). When we remain united to Christ, His life flows into us, like the sap in a grapevine flows from the vine into the branches. The result in the spiritual life is the same as in the vineyard: fruit, more fruit, and much fruit.

If you want your spiritual life to be useful, stay joined to Jesus. People desperately need your gifts, but they'll appreciate them more with a healthy dose of fruit.

Heavenly Father,

I want to manifest the spiritual gifts You have given me and spiritual fruit as well. Cleanse me and fill me with Your Holy Spirit. Amen.

———— *For the rest of your life . . .* ————

*give the Holy Spirit freedom to cultivate
the character of Christ in you.*

43

WHEN GOD CALLS

*The LORD had said to Abram, "Leave your country . . .
and go to the land I will show you."*

GENESIS 12:1

The American Red Cross has become such a part of the fabric of our nation's life that we take it for granted. But the huge organization we know today that accomplishes so much good for so many people exists because of the inspiration of one woman, Clara Barton.

Visiting Europe after the American Civil War, Barton came in contact with the Swiss-inspired International Red Cross society. Returning home, she set out to found an American chapter of the Red Cross society, doing so with a few friends on May 21, 1881. She led the American Red Cross in a volunteer capacity for twenty-three years. During that time the organization established a pattern for responding to disasters and providing relief to American military servicemen and the war-injured. Today the American Red Cross provides a vast array of physical, medical, and emotional support to our world—all because one woman saw a need and decided she could do something about it.

God almost always starts big things from little things. Think of Abraham being called to leave his country, Moses being called out of the wilderness to deliver a message to Egypt, David being called while a shepherd, Mary being called while a teenager. And in our day the son of a farmer becomes the world's most famous evangelist (Billy Graham); a tiny Albanian girl becomes the best-known servant of the poor (Mother Teresa); and a convicted felon becomes the leading minister to prisoners (Charles Colson).

God is constantly looking for and calling people into His service "whose hearts are fully committed to him" (2 Chron. 16:9). Our challenge is to believe that the smallest opportunity might become a key to unlocking something that could change the lives of multitudes of people. Granted, the size to which a project grows is not the point. Faithfulness is. And we are called to be faithful to minister to others, whether it's one person or a million.

Be sensitive to the opportunities that come your way, and be faithful to say yes when you sense God is calling. You have to take hold of the key in order to open the door.

Heavenly Father,

I know You have given me gifts and abilities, and I know there are needs all around me. Please show me where I can make a difference. Amen.

———————— *For the rest of your life . . .* ————————

prepare to do something big for God by being willing to do little things for Him.

44

REAPING WHAT WE SOW

Remember this: Whoever sows sparingly will also reap sparingly, and whoever sows generously will also reap generously.

2 CORINTHIANS 9:6

God has blessed you to be a blessing to others. He expects you to exercise good stewardship in those areas where you have been blessed—whether you are blessed materially, financially, or with certain talents and abilities, "from everyone who has been given much, much will be demanded" (Luke 12:48).

But sometimes our blessings can get in the way of our generosity; they can bring out the selfishness in us. If we don't use our gifts for others, those gifts may begin to dissipate. What goes around may come around. As Christ said, "If anyone does not remain in me, he is like a branch that is thrown away and withers" (John 15:6).

Sowing begins in the heart. It springs up out of love and gratitude and cannot help itself. It's the natural response of one who has a heart for God. The generous child of God realizes that all he has was given to him by God and is to be used for His purposes. Our tendency is to hold tightly to our blessings, thinking that they were given for our benefit. We think maybe we deserve them in some way, or maybe we earned them. But in reality everything we are, and all that we have, is a gift from the Great Giver.

When it comes to giving (or sowing), we sometimes make excuses by only giving "what we can afford" or by doing "what we are capable of." But what we can afford or what we can do is often based on the standard of living or limitations we ourselves have established. God will provide for our needs. He asks only that we give with a joyful heart.

When God calls us out of our comfort zone to give beyond what we think we can (see 2 Cor. 8:3), it's not because He wants us to have less but because He wants to give us more. If we hold back, we limit the harvest that comes from our sowing. But when we take God at His Word, we sow generously and reap abundantly. The next time you are asked to give of yourself or your resources, instead of taking the safe road, dig deep from within the pockets of a grateful heart and trust God for a harvest both now and in eternity.

Heavenly Father,

Help me learn to live within Your economy, not mine; to let my giving be a measure of Your generosity and resources, not mine. Amen.

──────── *For the rest of your life . . .* ────────

don't limit your own blessings by failing to be a blessing to others.

45

UNWORTHY TO SERVE

*"Your guilt is taken away and your sin atoned for." Then
I heard the voice of the Lord saying, "Whom shall
I Send?" . . . And I said, "Here am I. Send me!"*

ISAIAH 6:7–8

*U*nworthiness . . . low self-esteem . . . shame over sin. All of us have wrestled with thinking we were unworthy to be used by God. The prophet Isaiah certainly felt that way.

Isaiah's problem was thinking he was too sinful to serve a holy God. But when God revealed Himself to Isaiah and touched him with a personal call to serve, the prophet realized he was cleansed. When his life changed, he began to comprehend things from heaven he'd never understood before. He heard God saying, "Whom shall I send? And who will go for us?" Isaiah's hand shot up like a first-grader who couldn't wait to be chosen for the assignment: "Here am I. Send me!" (Isa. 6:8).

Every fall when our Bible study starts back, my heart melts over the many voices singing, "Here I am, Lord," and the number of volunteers who raise their hand to take care of the various details needed to run our ministry. Many feel unequipped or inadequate, and yet they are still willing to be used by God. All of us are too sinful to serve God when our frail humanity is measured against His perfection. Yet because of His grace, God comes to us afresh each season of our life—each day, each moment—and He offers cleansing. As we confess and seek forgiveness, He points us in a new direction.

When we receive His cleansing and obey His call, we begin to see and hear new things. Are we too self-centered or too busy to serve others? Absolutely. But if we say yes to God's cleansing, He will change our earthly interests to heavenly ones. Plus, we'll be given the opportunity to fellowship with Jesus and see Him work through us.

When you see a need, listen closely. Jesus is going to meet that need, but He may be calling you to go with Him and be His hands. If you raise your hand, He'll take yours in His, and you can go together. Be sure to open your eyes so you don't miss the things you've never seen before.

Heavenly Father,

I am truly sorry for all my sins. But I am so thankful that You have washed me clean—made me whiter than snow—so that I can serve You with joy and a clear conscience the rest of my life. Amen.

———— *For the rest of your life . . .* ————

cultivate the discipline of seeing yourself
and your opportunities through God's eyes.

46

LIVING SACRIFICES

*Therefore, I urge you, brothers, in view of God's mercy,
to offer your bodies as living sacrifices, holy and
pleasing to God—this is your spiritual act of worship.*

ROMANS 12:1

hat does God mean when He asks us to give our bodies as a living sacrifice? Can we die as a sacrifice and yet remain alive? In a spiritual sense, yes.

Old Testament Jews knew all about sacrifices and offerings. Virtually every aspect of life, whether secular or spiritual, was tied into Israel's system of worship. Sacrificial animals (often an unblemished lamb) were placed on the altar and consumed by fire. They were intended to express the worshipper's total dedication and consecration, and they brought reconciliation with God. In the New Testament, Christ, the Lamb of God (see John 1:29), gave Himself as a sacrificial offering in complete consecration and surrender to the will of God. Because He was sinless, He did not need reconciliation with God. His sacrifice was intended to reconcile mankind to God.

In light of the sacrifice that Christ made for us, we are exhorted today to make our own offering. We are to offer our body—which represents the sum total of who we are, all that we have, and all that we do. Unlike the Old Testament believers who offered animals, we are to offer ourselves as living sacrifices to be consumed and used by God for His glory.

Offering ourselves to God is not just giving up our spare evenings or a Sunday morning but the whole of our lives to Him. It means giving up our plans, our money, our family—everything that has any significance at all to us. Everything is given over to Him, entrusted completely into His care.

If we claim to be followers of Christ while holding on to certain areas of our life, we have not understood that the fully surrendered life is to be the norm for every Christian. It is a process of a daily sacrificing of who we are and what we do in order to live in complete dependence on the One who sacrificed so much for us.

Heavenly Father,

In view of Your mercy toward me, I offer myself afresh to You as a living sacrifice. Spend my life in Your service as You see fit. Amen.

—————— For the rest of your life . . . ——————

choose to remain a living sacrifice by remaining on the altar even when the fires of life get hot.

47

THE PORTRAIT OF
A FAITHFUL WOMAN

"I am the Lord's servant," Mary answered.
"May it be to me as you have said."
LUKE 1:38

*I*n both the Old and New Testaments, God intervened in human affairs by sending angels to speak with people. That's not the norm today, but what if it were? What would you do if an angel appeared to you with a message from God? About nine months before Jesus was born, an angel appeared to a young Jewish girl with a life-changing assignment.

When the angel Gabriel appeared to her, Mary said, "Your word is my command." She didn't know the challenges she would face as the mother of Jesus, but she said yes anyway. She believed that whatever God called her to do, He would provide the ability for her to do. She had an attitude of trust that allowed her to respond in faith to God's request. It's not hard to see why Mary was "highly favored" by the Lord.

Saying yes to God brings blessings, but it also brings pain. God wants to know that we are faithful not only at the beginning of our calling but at the end as well. Therefore, He told Mary that a sword would pierce her soul as a result of raising Jesus to fulfill His own calling from God (Luke 2:35). Throughout Jesus' life, Mary's heart was pierced time and again as her faith was tested and her commitment challenged. While there were periods of doubt and confusion, she remained faithful throughout her life.

Mary endured a number of piercings through which she demonstrated her faithfulness to God: she endured the shame of becoming pregnant out of wedlock; she kept her knowledge about Jesus' identity secret until His public ministry; she had to submit her motherly emotions to God's plan for her son; and she watched her son as He was rejected and killed by those He was trying to help.

Mary is a model for Christian women today. We may never hear personally from Gabriel, but may the attitude of our heart be like Mary's: "I am the Lord's servant. May it be to me as you have said."

Heavenly Father,

I know there may be times when I'm not listening for Your voice. Please help me to hear. Speak however loudly You must. I want to say yes to You. Amen.

For the rest of your life . . .

don't "accidentally" say no to God by failing to say yes.

99

48

BEING BORN AGAIN

*"I tell you the truth, no one can see the kingdom
of God unless he is born again."*
JOHN 3:3

*A*lmost everyone has been approached by someone witnessing on the street who asked, point-blank, "Have you been born again?" If you're not a Christian when that happens, you probably think the person is a little strange. In fact, you might have the same question that Nicodemus put to Jesus: "What do you mean, 'born again'?" (see John 3:4).

The words Jesus used to describe salvation and conversion can be confusing, intimidating, and unclear to a non-Christian. What the words describe, however, is nothing short of life-changing.

To be born again, or to be born of the Spirit, is to be regenerated by God. In the Old Testament, God speaks of giving Israel a new birth (see Isa. 66:7). In the New Testament, Jesus uses physical birth as a metaphor for what it means to enter into spiritual life with God. When we place our trust in Jesus as Lord and Savior, we are born again and become a child of God. Infants do not see the physical world until they are born. Similarly no one can see the kingdom of God until they experience spiritual rebirth. Infants are born with a potential that they realize as they grow and mature. Likewise those who come by faith into a relationship with God must grow as Christians.

With this new life we have a new Father, a new family, a new home, and a new identity. While our outer characteristics are the same, an inner transformation begins as we develop new desires and new attitudes toward people. We begin to view everything around us from God's perspective. And relationships are more important than responsibilities.

My attitude now is quite different from years ago. Next time someone asks me the "Are you born again?" question, I will respond differently. With a grateful heart, I will give a resounding "Yes!" and say a prayer of thanks to the Birth-giver. What will you say when someone asks you?

Heavenly Father,

Thank You for providing the new birth; thank You that I am born again through faith in Jesus. Help me to grow up in Him, to become the new creation You have made me. Amen.

——— *For the rest of your life . . .* ———

let "born again" be the gateway to the kingdom of God, not a religious cliché.

49

GOD'S WILL
FOR YOUR LIFE

*"Love the Lord your God with all your heart and with all
your soul and with all your mind and
with all your strength."*

MARK 12:30

One day a member of our Bible class stopped me in the hall-way of our church. She had been delayed and missed the meeting.

"Nancy, I heard today's lesson was on discovering God's will."

"That's right."

"Well, what is it?"

"What is what?"

"What is God's will?"

"Well . . . His will is for you to spend time getting to know Him better and to love Him more."

With a look of disappointment, she said, "That's it? I mean, that's all? There's no plan, no pointers, no special tips on what I should do specifically?" I understood how she felt.

Mankind has always wanted to do something to earn the love of God instead of loving God for what He has already done.

We want a plan, but God gives us a process. We want a program, but He gives us a person. We want a formula, but He provides a relationship. Simply put, God's will is not an end in itself; it is a means whereby we get to know Him better.

God said, "For I know the plans I have for you . . . plans to give you hope and a future" (Jer. 29:11). Jesus knows where He wants to take you. He is much more interested in your doing His will than you are. But the way to discover God's individual will (how to be useful in His kingdom) for your life is by focusing on His universal will (loving Him and others). In John 17:3, Jesus said, "Now this is eternal life [God's will for abundant living]: that they may know you, the only true God, and Jesus Christ, whom you have sent." If you will follow Jesus one day at a time—through prayer, Bible study, and being with other believers—you will come to know Him and know yourself better as well.

As you "seek first his kingdom and his righteousness," everything else will be added to you (Matt. 6:33)—including the peace that you are in fact living in God's will.

Heavenly Father,

Forgive me for seeking Your will for me more than I seek You. Help me to know that You will guide my steps as I trust in You with all my heart. Amen.

——————— *For the rest of your life . . .* ———————

*when you wonder about God's will,
focus afresh on loving God.*

SPLIT PERSONALITY

I do not understand what I do. For what I want to do I do
not do, but what I hate I do. . . . For I have the desire to
do what is good, but I cannot carry it out. . . . Who will
rescue me from this body of death? Thanks be to God—
through Jesus Christ our Lord!

ROMANS 7:15, 18, 24–25

ost Christians struggle with a spiritual split personality. No sooner do we think we are on the road to doing good than we discover "evil is right there with [us]" (Rom. 7:21). Our spirit wants to speak well of others, but our sinful flesh is drawn toward gossip. Our spirit wants to give to those in need, but our sinful flesh grasps what is ours. Our spirit wants to follow Christ, but our flesh wants to go its own way. It seems at every corner we come face-to-face with our counterpart, the sinful self.

We cannot win this war on our own—and it is a war. Paul says the spirit and the flesh "are in conflict with each other" (Gal. 5:17). But he also said if we "live by the Spirit," we will not carry out the desires of the flesh (Gal. 5:16). The answer to our struggle is to let Christ lead the way, to follow His Holy Spirit every day. If we give Him all our temptations, "he who began a good work in [us] will carry it on to completion until the day of Christ

Jesus" (Phil. 1:6). As believers in Christ, we did not receive a spirit that makes us a slave to fear, but we "received the Spirit of sonship" (Rom. 8:15). "If God is for us, who can be against us?" (v. 31). In all things (including our own sinful ways), "we are more than conquerors" through Christ (v. 37).

Our spiritual split personality has an upside: it makes us grateful. When we see who we are in our fleshly nature, it makes us so grateful for who Christ is. When we see our sins, we are grateful for our Savior. When we struggle, we are grateful that God's new birth has given us an awareness of righteousness. (How terrible would it be to live perfectly content with the sins of the flesh?) And when we confess our sins, we are grateful to be the children of a loving Father who forgives us (see 1 John 1:9).

Yes, every Christian has a spiritual split personality. But we know that by the power of God's Spirit we are becoming one with Christ more and more each day.

Heavenly Father,

Thank You for forgiving me when I yield to my flesh. Help me to stay focused on Christ by being filled with the Spirit, moment by moment. Amen.

—— *For the rest of your life . . .* ——

focus on Christ's perfection rather than your imperfection.

THE PERFECT MATE

*There is a time for everything, and a season
for every activity under heaven.*
ECCLESIASTES 3:1

No one wants to be alone in this world, and God does not want us to *feel* alone either. Sometimes, though, we find ourselves without a life partner at a time we wish we had one. Perhaps we've never been married or are newly single as a widow or one divorced. The thought of finding someone to share life with seems overwhelming if not unlikely.

Fortunately we serve a God who loves to accomplish what seems overwhelming and unlikely to us. Instead of fearing that we're too set in our ways to find a life partner, God wants us to be set in His ways and begin to pray. Where does it say in the Bible we shouldn't pray for a life partner?

In Genesis 2:18 God said, "It is not good for the man to be alone. I will make a helper suitable for him." God also said in Jeremiah 29:11, "For I know the plans I have for you . . . plans to prosper you and not to harm you, plans to give you hope and a future." So never give up on God; He has a plan.

Remember that Sarah, Abraham's wife, thought she was too old to conceive, but God proved her wrong. God's ways are different from and higher than our ways (see Isa. 55:8–9). We must wait on God, "for he who promised is faithful" (Heb. 10:23).

While God certainly does call certain individuals to a life of singleness (which has the advantage of single-minded devotion to God; see 1 Cor. 7:32–34), marriage is the norm for most. That which is the norm in God's sight, therefore, is something to pray for and seek, trusting in His guidance and provision. What is even more important to God, however, than your being united with someone, is for you to be united with Him. In fact, He wants to be sure of that for both you and your potential partner. Then your union will be successfully centered on Christ (see Eph. 5:22–33).

If finding a mate seems like an impossibility, pray boldly for God's perfect timing and God's perfect plan. For with Him all things *are* possible (see Matt. 19:26), including a perfect mate.

Heavenly Father,

Remind all who are single in this world that they are never alone, that there is no better companion in this life than You. Amen.

———— *For the rest of your life . . .* ————

live in God's provision for the impossible each day.

TRAVELING LIGHT

*"Take my yoke upon you. . . . For my yoke is
easy and my burden is light."*
MATTHEW 11:29–30

When our children were old enough for us to begin taking
longer family vacations, there were four females and two
males in our group. Guess which four brought the most luggage?
And guess which two ended up carrying most of it? Over time
my daughters and I learned the skills of traveling light, and my
husband and son were grateful. All journeys are more enjoyable
the less baggage we choose to drag along with us.

That is definitely true in the Christian life: the less baggage
from our past we drag behind us, the more enjoyable our journey
toward heaven will be. Fear, doubt, wounds, unforgiveness, hurt
feelings . . . these and other pieces of emotional baggage from
our past make our spiritual journey so burdensome. Jesus invites
us to exchange all our weighty "stuff" for His light "load"—
"my yoke is easy and my burden is light." If we will drop our baggage at His feet and take on His yoke, we will find that walking
in tandem with Him is lighter than we could have imagined.

A daily question for every Christian is, how much baggage
from the past are you carrying? A maturing Christian learns

that life in the Spirit (see Rom. 8:2) is a life of freedom, not of burdens. Yes, there are responsibilities but not burdens heaped on our backs that we cannot shake off. We don't live with the burdens of dos and don'ts or of past failures. Instead we live in the freedom of knowing Christ. He forgives our sins (takes the burdens off our back) and fills us with motivation and desire for obeying God's commands.

When we keep our baggage and try to carry it ourselves, we are constrained, like being bound with chains. The Christian life is not about what we can't do ourselves but what we can do in Christ. It was for freedom that Christ came to loose us from the past and welcome us into the future (see Gal. 5:1). It's the difference between dragging an old-fashioned heavy trunk behind us or carrying a light canvas bag slung over one shoulder.

Start today's leg of your journey by giving your baggage to Jesus and taking His yoke upon you. There's nothing you'll need that He won't supply.

Heavenly Father,

Forgive me for holding on to my baggage from the past. I give it up to Jesus today. Show me how to take His yoke upon me today and every day. Amen.

—————— For the rest of your life . . . ——————

practice the discipline of releasing your baggage to Jesus the moment you realize you've picked it up.

53

FORGIVING
AND FORGIVEN

*"For if you forgive men when they sin against you, your
heavenly Father will also forgive you. But if
you do not forgive men their sins, your Father
will not forgive your sins."*

MATTHEW 6:14–15

C. S. Lewis wrote, "Everyone says forgiveness is a lovely idea until they have something to forgive." How could he know me so well? If someone has done me wrong (or especially if someone has wronged my children), my natural self would much rather harbor a grudge than forgive. Somehow I enjoy the power of hurting them back, if ever so slightly, by thinking bad thoughts of them or purposely ignoring them. In reality I am only hurting myself because of the consequence of unforgiveness.

I remember calling my father once to complain that a coach was not giving my child enough playing time in a sport (typical overbearing parent). Because of a poor connection, it was impossible for us to converse. "Call me back later when you have a clear signal," he said. Before calling him back, I had some time to think. I could feel God giving me a chilling illustration. There was no doubt that God, like my father, would love to listen to my prayers. But when the cloud of unforgiveness looms in the air, there is definitely not a clear signal.

When we hold grudges against others, we block the communication between ourselves and God. The Bible tells us to forgive whatever grievances we may have against others, and to forgive as the Lord forgave us (see Col. 3:13). We do not enjoy the Lord's forgiveness when we refuse to forgive others (see Matt. 6:14–15). Even the apostle Peter asked Jesus, "Lord, how many times shall I forgive my brother when he sins against me? Up to seven times?" He probably thought seven was going above and beyond the call of duty, but Jesus said, "I tell you, not seven times, but seventy-seven times"—that is, don't put a limit on how often you forgive (Matt. 18:21–22).

If I sense static on the line when I talk to God, one of the first things I am learning to check is whether I am holding a grudge against anyone. If so, I take care of that first and call back with a clear connection.

Heavenly Father,

I could never begin to count the number of times You have forgiven me. So please help me not to count the times I forgive others. Help me forgive as I am forgiven. Amen.

———— For the rest of your life . . . ————

*gauge your willingness to forgive
by your gratitude for having been forgiven.*

111

54

NEVER MEET
A STRANGER

*The Samaritan woman said to him, "You are a Jew and
I am a Samaritan woman. How can you ask me for a
drink?" (For Jews do not associate with Samaritans.)*

JOHN 4:9

*I*t has been said that the true measure of a person is how
they treat someone they hardly know. This idea has its
root in the Golden Rule—treating others the way we'd like to
be treated—and Jesus' second great commandment, "Love your
neighbor as yourself." It's the message in the story of the Good
Samaritan, and why Jesus commended so highly the Samaritan
who helped a stranger, instead of the two religious leaders who
turned away from the needs of their countryman.

My youngest daughter is the kind of person who never meets
a stranger. She has been loved so much by so many for so long
that she just naturally loves everybody else and assumes they love
her. She genuinely looks each person in the eye and really cares
what he or she thinks, no matter who they are. Unfortunately she
is the exception in our culture, not the rule. We are either too
busy with our agenda or only interested in those who are like us

or can help us. Helping a neighbor becomes more of a nuisance than a pleasure. And isolation becomes easier and requires less effort in a world that is already spread too thin.

Jesus also never met a stranger, even when the custom of the day was not to talk to certain people like Samaritans—especially a Samaritan woman. Everywhere Jesus went He cared about people no matter who they were—lepers or blind or of another culture. He truly loved them and wanted to know what they thought. Jesus came into this world to serve and care about others, and we are to have the same attitude as He had (see Phil. 2:5–7). Spending time in the Father's Word learning how much we are loved and cared for should overflow to our relationship with others.

How many strangers do you meet every day? Make it a goal not to meet any. Taking time to show all the people you meet that they are truly important will reflect how Jesus felt about you the first time the two of you met.

Heavenly Father,

Please create in me a loving heart. Teach me to listen, not talk; to give, not take; and to care, not ignore. Amen.

For the rest of your life . . .

consider every new person you meet a friend you're meeting for the first time.

55

THE DIVINE COACH

And we know that in all things God works
for the good of those who love him, who
have been called according to his purpose.

ROMANS 8:28

In the life of a Christian, there is no such thing as chance. God has ordained every circumstance. But most often we believe we are in control of our circumstances. We think we have caused both the good and the bad in our lives. And when faced with a crisis, we cry out to God for help and then wonder why He allowed this trial to happen. But God allows everything we go through for a higher purpose.

I have heard it said, "If you want to hear God laugh, just tell Him your plans." And Proverbs says, "In his heart a man plans his course, but the LORD determines his steps" (16:9). It's not that the choices we make don't matter; they do. And it's not that we are puppets with no say; we're not. But somehow in God's mysterious ways, He is able to incorporate our choices with His ultimate plan. It's kind of like having an invisible coach in the basketball game of life. God, the Coach, wants us to make the right moves, but sometimes we don't. And when we don't, He may change the flow of the game in order to work around our choices. No matter what moves we make, with God as Coach, you *will* win the game.

The idea that God ordains everything that comes to us is profoundly life changing. If we believe that God loves us, and nothing can separate us from His love (see Rom. 8:38–39), why do we worry? Why be so concerned with the future? Would it not be better to live in gratitude for a divine Coach who promises us that He will work everything for good that comes into our life?

This one thing I know: I cannot play this game of life unless I read the Rule Book. I won't even understand what the Coach is trying to tell me. Just like the athlete who trains to win, I need to spend time every day training to live the Christian life. I need to be on my knees in prayer and listening to the Coach, getting His instructions on how to play the game. I may not always follow His instructions as carefully as I should, but I know He will cause victory to be mine in the end.

Heavenly Father,

Thank You that everything that comes into my life has been filtered through Your loving hands—even the difficult times of life. Amen.

For the rest of your life . . .

welcome every play of life as part of the divine plan.

56

GIANTS IN YOUR LAND

"And do not be afraid of the people of the land. . . .
Their protection is gone, but the LORD is with us.
Do not be afraid of them."

NUMBERS 14:9

There they were, ready to open the great gift they had been given . . . and they got cold feet. I am referring to the nation of Israel, and you doubtless remember the story. God had promised His people a homeland in Canaan after four hundred years of slavery in Egypt. Moses sent a party of twelve spies into the land to scout it out and bring back a report. He could hardly hear the good report of Joshua and Caleb for the rattling of the other ten spies' knees knocking together out of fear!

What were they so afraid of? Giants in the land . . . walled cities . . . armies with chariots. Here they were, a bunch of ragtags who had never been in a battle. They had no weapons, no strategy, no strength. How could they defeat the armies of the Canaanite giants? Were Joshua and Caleb wishful thinkers, or did they know something the other ten spies didn't? They knew what we must know if we are going to defeat the giants in our land: God makes no promises He does not keep. God had promised that land to Israel's forefather, Abraham (see Gen. 12:7).

All Israel had to do to inherit the land, which included defeating the giants, was believe God and follow His lead.

That's all we have to do to defeat our giants as well. Here are some of the giants that we are fearful of: an unsaved spouse, a wayward child, elderly parents in need of support, limited finances, unemployment, growing old, health problems, lack of self-appreciation. These are real—but they're not worth giving up the gift of God for. They must be engaged by faith and driven off your land—the land of your heart where the fruit of the Spirit is to grow in abundance (see Gal. 5:22–23).

God has promised you peace and joy on this earth. But He did not say obtaining it would be battle-free. Our part is to strap on our spiritual armor (see Eph. 6:11–18) and engage the giants by faith. God's part is to provide the victory He has promised.

Heavenly Father,

There are giants in my land and on my horizon—and some of them are fearful to me. Give me the faith of Joshua and Caleb to submit my fears to Your promises. Amen.

For the rest of your life . . .

measure every giant you face against the promises of God's Word.

57

HOPE WHEN LIFE
LOOKS HOPELESS

*Yet this I call to mind and therefore I have hope: Because
of the LORD's great love we are not consumed, for his
compassions never fail. They are new every
morning; great is your faithfulness.*
LAMENTATIONS 3:21–23

Today there are many people around the world for whom
every day is an intense struggle, if not for survival at least for
hope. While for most of us paying bills, getting physical check-
ups, and balancing a social life is the norm; for others poverty,
disease, and persecution are the routine.

I remember one great biblical leader who was rejected by his
friends, his family, his coworkers, even the ruler of his nation.
He was ultimately imprisoned and died a martyr's death, never
seeing any of the fruit of the labor of his faithful life. It's hard
for most of us to relate to such realities—to live with such painful obstacles every day, to find relief only in death. It's amazing
to me that this person who lived with such trials also wrote,
"Therefore I have hope" (Lam. 3:21). Jeremiah the prophet was
a hopeful man in a hopeless situation.

Defining hope is key. It is not the sort of wishful thinking our lives are full of: "I hope the economy improves"; "I hope it doesn't rain tomorrow"; "I hope my child makes the honor roll." Those statements express hope of a sort but not biblical hope. Biblical hope is akin to biblical faith: "Now faith is being sure of what we hope for and certain of what we do not see" (Heb. 11:1).

Jeremiah's hope was not wishful thinking; it was evidence of things not seen. He had hope because of the Lord's great love . . . [because] His compassions never fail . . . [because] they are new every morning . . . [because] God's faithfulness is great. Biblical hope is based on the character of God . . . not a circumstance or human ability.

If you are in a situation that seems hopeless, be a person of hope by maintaining certainty about God, His compassions, His mercies, and His faithfulness. Your situation may seem hopeless, but that doesn't mean you have to be.

Heavenly Father,

I am thankful there is always hope where You are concerned. In circumstances that seem hopeless, help me keep my eyes on You, the God of hope. Amen.

———— *For the rest of your life . . .* ————

cultivate hope by getting to know the certainty of God's character.

58

A HUNGER FOR HUMILITY

"For whoever exalts himself will be humbled, and
whoever humbles himself will be exalted."
MATTHEW 23:12

*H*ave you noticed that the longer you walk with God, the
more aware you become of your sinful nature? Pride, especially, rears its ugly head when I least expect it. It's the hardest
part of the old self to give up. It is deeply ingrained in our flesh
and surfaces at the slightest urging. But for the children of God,
there is a hunger deep within to obtain full victory in this area
of our life.

As Christians, we know God desires that we walk humbly
with Him. It is the only way He can make any progress with our
inner life. To humble yourself does not mean to belittle yourself.
It means to see yourself through God's eyes; to allow Him to
shine His light on the dark corners of your life so the need for
change can be seen. God is the One (through the Holy Spirit)
who does the changing. Humility (through confession) opens
the door for the Holy Spirit to begin His work, enabling us to
embrace our absolute dependence on God for everything.

Have you been stressed out lately? Have you been afraid
to show your true feelings? Pride will insist that you remain in

control. It can cause utter exhaustion and weariness. There is a constant concern of being "found out"; of having our weaknesses revealed. But the more we hide our weaknesses, the stronger their hold on our lives. Where pride sees no need for change, humility longs for it.

Humility is what brings the strength of God into our lives. It is the cure for the cancer of self-absorption. It opens the way for God's power and grace. As long as you refuse to acknowledge your weaknesses, you will never know what it means to experience true joy and freedom in Christ. Remember God opposes the proud but gives grace to the humble (see James 4:6). So why not humble yourself now to receive His grace? He will exalt your weaknesses by revealing His strength and glory through them.

Don't wait until one day your pride may be revealed and you may be humbled as never before. Let humility draw you closer to Christ now and show you the way to experience total freedom in this life.

Heavenly Father,

I confess that I am sometimes consumed with the pride of my life. Please forgive me. I want to have a humble heart before You, knowing that You oppose the proud but give grace to the humble. Amen.

———— *For the rest of your life . . .* ————

increase in humility by submitting to God's will not by seeking to be humble.

59

USING YOUR GIFTS

It was he who gave some to be apostles, some to be prophets, some to be evangelists, and some to be pastors and teachers, to prepare God's people for works of service, so that the body of Christ may be built up until we all reach unity in the faith and in the knowledge of the Son of God and become mature, attaining to the whole measure to the fullness of Christ.

EPHESIANS 4:11–13

God has given every believer one or more spiritual gifts, but they are not for our benefit. They are for the benefit of His people. Just as Christ is the Vine and we are the branches (see John 15:5), likewise our gifts (given to us by the Holy Spirit) are not for display but to be given away. Spiritual gifts are for the purpose of building up the body of believers, not for building up the stature or reputation of individuals (see 1 Cor. 14:12).

If you are not sure what your gifts are, get involved in helping others. Serve in your church or community and find out how others are built up and encouraged by you. What do you enjoy doing? In what ways have you been affirmed by what you do? Once you begin to discover your gifts, it's important to examine your motives. Am I bringing glory to God through what I do or glory to myself? Do I genuinely care about helping others grow in Christ or only about my own growth?

In my Bible study, numerous women serve in various capacities. Not only am I personally edified by these women, but I enjoy watching how Christ reveals Himself through each one as they use and develop their gifts. Within this faithful group of servants, you can find all the gifts functioning that are needed to keep a large ministry going: administration, helping, encouragement, intercession, teaching, and others. What is most clear is that every person's contribution is necessary to the growth of the women in our ministry. God touches many lives as each woman exercises the gift(s) He has given her.

And God wants to make a difference through you wherever you are right now. Are you allowing your surroundings to determine how to invest your life, or are you practicing God's presence by serving others with your gift(s) and trusting Him to lead you to your own place of service?

If your deep desire is to bring glory to God, the best place to begin is by using the very gift(s) He gave you for that purpose.

Heavenly Father,

I want to be used for Your glory. Please help me discover and polish the gift(s) You have given me that I might serve Your church. Amen.

———— *For the rest of your life . . .* ————

use the gifts of God in you to bring glory to God through you.

How's Your Hearing?

"Speak, LORD, for your servant is listening."
1 SAMUEL 3:9

*M*y grandmother lived in a nursing home near the end of her life, and the fact that she didn't see well and could only hear in one ear made for interesting visits. I would get near her good ear and yell out, "Hey Granny, it's me, Nancy!" And from across the room another elderly lady would call out, "Hey there, I am so glad you are here!"

We all expect our physical hearing to get weaker as we age—perhaps disappear altogether. But our spiritual hearing is just the opposite. It ought to get better the older we become in the Lord. In the early days of cell phones, it was common to see people struggling to maintain a good connection when talking. As technology has improved, so has cell-phone communication. It should be the same with us as we grow in the Lord: our ability to "hear" God should get better the longer we walk with Him.

How *do* we hear from God? In biblical days, before the Word of God had been brought together in the Bible, God sometimes spoke audibly. For instance, he called out to the young boy Samuel several times before the child realized it was God speaking audibly to him.

Today God speaks to us primarily through His Word as the Holy Spirit illumines our heart to understand what the Bible says, "Your word is a lamp to my feet and a light for my path" (Ps. 119:105).

God can also speak to us as we pray. We have to be careful to confirm the impressions we get in prayer with Scripture or through godly counsel. But rather than fearing we might misunderstand God and make a mistake, we should approach prayer with a listening ear: "Speak, LORD, for your servant is listening." God can also speak or guide us through the circumstances of our lives, though not every open door comes from God.

Finally, God can speak to us through friends, authorities, and counselors. Others in whom the Holy Spirit lives may be used by God to direct our path. Again, we must be equally eager to hear and to confirm. So, how's your hearing? Has your ability to hear God improved as you've grown with Him?

Heavenly Father,

I am so thankful You want to talk to me. Help me to stop talking long enough to be able to hear Your voice. Amen.

For the rest of your life . . .

the more you want to hear God's voice,
the more you likely will.

61

WALKING THROUGH
THE VALLEY

*Even though I walk through the valley of the shadow
of death, I will fear no evil, for you are with me.*

PSALM 23:4

*D*eath always throws us into the valley . . . the place we least desire to go and when we least expect to go. It comes as a thief in the night, and steals away those we love, leaving us to mourn and grieve. Where before we stood on the mountaintop where the light in our lives had shined so brightly, now a cloud is cast over all that we do.

Whether you have lost someone you loved, or you are faced with your own mortality, death can be devastating. When we walk through death's valley, we come face-to-face with fear, and life seems suddenly to stop. Our soul is overwhelmed, our heart is broken, and we can barely walk, talk, or listen . . . much less carry on the routine of life.

Yet in that valley we can choose to respond with a steadfast determination that shouts to the Lord, "I will fear no evil, for you are with me" (Ps. 23:4). "There is nothing that can separate me from your love" (see Rom. 8:38–39). "You have promised always to be with me" (see Heb. 13:5). The claim of God's promises brings light into a valley where all has grown dim.

For life is not what it seems. We may think we are alone, but God is with us. Loss is terrible but not forever. Death seems permanent but is only temporary. Jesus died but was raised again. The power of the resurrection takes on a new meaning when we face our own crucifixions.

Saying good-bye to loved ones is excruciatingly painful. But slowly and most assuredly, God provides comfort and brings light back into our lives. He leads us out of the valley and back onto the mountaintop where the view becomes crystal clear again.

We need not fear death, for Christ has conquered death in His resurrection. Death may separate us for a time, but Christ will reunite us forever.

Heavenly Father,

Thank You for the promise that death has been overcome in Christ. May I never again fear the prospect or the fact of death, but view it as a doorway to eternity with You. Amen.

For the rest of your life . . .

view death as the last enemy conquered by Christ.

127

62

Spiritual Warfare

In order that Satan might not outwit us.
For we are not unaware of his schemes.

2 CORINTHIANS 2:11

When you hear the words "red suit, pointed tail, horns, and a pitchfork," you think I'm describing the devil, right? Wrong. What I'm describing is the world's caricature of the devil. The danger of seeing that image as a joke, which it is, is that we may also begin to think of Satan's work as a joke, which it isn't. Spiritual warfare is reality, not fantasy.

On the day of Christ's death and resurrection, a decisive battle was won. God defeated Satan, who had done his best to destroy God's plans. But he could not overcome God's power. In spite of God's victory, the war continues. Even though we know the outcome of the war—Satan will one day be defeated for good—we must prepare every day for battle so that we don't get swept up in Satan's deceitful ways.

How does he deceive us? The obvious ways—theft, greed, lying, and the like—are not what trip me up. It's the subtle ways where he can be most dangerous. He loves to appeal to those areas where we are most vulnerable.

Are you a Bible teacher? Don't let knowledge "puff [you] up" (see 1 Cor. 8:1). Are you involved in fund-raising for charity? Don't envy someone else's resources. Are you a mom taking care of little ones? Don't let your physical exhaustion affect your spiritual character.

Satan will do anything to keep you from turning to God—discourage you, deceive you, and destroy you. While he cannot possess the believer in Christ, he can oppress the believer and have serious effects on the progress of a Christian's walk. When we pray to God and fill our minds with His Word, we walk in the light. Satan will always try to keep you in darkness and have you walk in fear.

But we have nothing to fear. He who is in us is greater than he who is in the world (see 1 John 4:4). God did not give us a spirit of fear but of love, power, and a sound mind (see 2 Tim. 1:7 NKJV). Remember: the enemy may be present in the battles, but God has won the war.

Heavenly Father,

You, living in me, is my ever-present defense against the deceit of the devil. Thank You for leading me not into temptation, for delivering me from the evil one. Amen.

For the rest of your life . . .

*don't fail to gain spiritual victory
by failing to enter the fight.*

63

THE HURRIED CHRISTIAN

*Wait for the LORD; be strong and take heart
and wait for the LORD.*

PSALM 27:14

Could you move along?" "I don't have time!" "What is taking so long?" "We are going to be late!" "Please hurry!" I cringe when I think how many of those exclamations I have used. Can you relate?

Our generation values "instant" everything—instant phone connections, instant food, instant messaging on the Internet . . . even instant religion. We want God to get in line with our other responsibilities and other "gods." We want Him to keep up with our deadlines and bring us immediate satisfaction. But as we plow forward, we discover that God's schedule doesn't always keep pace with our own driven desires. Before we know it, we begin to give up on God and start looking for better resources. There's only one problem: there are none.

God wants us to trade places and let Him lead the way. If we will wait on His guidance and trust in His timing, He will prove His faithfulness. No matter how slow-moving the hours, no matter how hopeless things may appear, God's outcome is always better.

Don't worry that others are moving ahead, even if they are getting instant results from other sources. We are trusting in the One true source that satisfies eternally. His results are worth the wait.

This attitude is not what you will see among the current generation. It goes against the tide of the hurried Christian whose life hardly seems different from those in the secular world—whose frantic lifestyles display little peace or patience. Waiting on God is the only way to receive the promises of God. And He promises a satisfaction that surpasses all the quick fixes of the world.

Heavenly Father,

I know You are neither early nor late but always on time. Please help me adjust my schedule to Yours. Help me to seek and find satisfaction in You and in Your time. Amen.

————— *For the rest of your life . . .* —————

*avoid disappointment in life by
living on God's timetable alone.*

64

CREATING A NEW YOU

He who began a good work in you . . .
PHILIPPIANS 1:6

A huge block of marble was given to a sculptor who began a carving and then stopped. The stone sat gathering dust for forty years until a young Michelangelo came along and saw David, the king of Israel, in the stone, waiting to be released. For two years Michelangelo chipped away at the stone, revealing more and more of David. On one occasion a small boy, after watching Michelangelo work, asked him, "How did you know he was in there?" Michelangelo replied, "I just took away everything that was not David."

That's what God is doing with us—chipping away everything that is not the image of Jesus. God's goal is to conform us to the image of His Son (see Rom. 8:29). While others (and we ourselves) may see us as nothing but a block of humanity, God sees something beneath the surface just waiting to be revealed. Like a master sculptor, He removes everything that stands in the way of Christ in us being released.

There's a difference between marble and flesh and blood. Marble does not fight the sculptor as he works. Marble yields to the sculptor's tools and takes on exactly the shape the sculptor desires. We are not so compliant. We may not like what God, the Sculptor, does to our flesh, our old nature, that must be removed. The Bible talks of mankind suppressing the work of God (see Rom. 1:18) and of Christians resisting the Holy Spirit (see Eph. 4:30; 1 Thess. 5:19). God will not force us into the image of Jesus. He wants us willingly to submit ourselves to His loving hands.

Our joyful obedience to Christ as Lord makes it possible for God to reveal Him through us. When we trust the Sculptor, we know that whatever He is doing *in* us is to make something more beautiful *of* us. God causes every stroke of His divine tools to work together to conform us to the image of Jesus (see Rom. 8:29).

Allow God the artist to have free reign with you, His subject. Only then can the Christ in you be set free.

Heavenly Father,

I confess afresh today that I am willing for You to chip away everything in my life that doesn't look like Jesus. Thank You for conforming me to His image. Amen.

——— *For the rest of your life . . .* ———

welcome the work of the Sculptor's tools
no matter how uncomfortable they may be.

65

WHAT REAL FAITH
LOOKS LIKE

I have fought the good fight. I have finished the race.
I have kept the faith.
2 TIMOTHY 4:7

*A*t a prayer service for a good friend, his wife rolled him into the chapel while our gathered Bible study community sat in silence. Many of us had known this man through the years as vibrant, strong, and energetic, a long-distance runner who lived the same way he ran—with his eyes on the future. But the man we greeted was weak, pale, bald—though never more handsome—and very much living in the moment. His recently diagnosed inoperable brain cancer had rapidly taken its toll. As I held a microphone for him, a tear rolled down his cheek while every ear strained to capture his failing speech:

> I want everyone to know that this is not about
> me. . . . it's about Jesus. There is nothing in your life
> more important than Him. I am in a win-win situa-
> tion. If He chooses to heal me, great. Otherwise,
> I get to be with Him. I am more blessed than anyone
> I know.

His words made me think of Paul's writing: "to live is Christ and to die is gain" (Phil. 1:21). I also thought of Jesus being submitted to God's will—"yet not my will, but yours be done" (Luke 22:42)—and saw that same humility in our friend.

His faith that day was the opposite of resignation and surrender. Instead of a cause for speculation or introspection, his faith was cause for gratitude and praise. He was grateful for the breath of life . . . grateful for precious time with loved ones . . . grateful for the gift of every hour that remained. Oh, to live each day like our faithful friend, not taking for granted this priceless gift we call "life." To live each day seeing God's strength in our weakness.

I believe Jesus Christ orchestrated that prayer service so He might speak to our faith family about living life with an eternal focus . . . about gratitude . . . about what real faith looks like. I wonder if He is speaking to you through my friend's words right now? God offers no guarantees about how life on this earth will end, only that it will. My friend's faith grew stronger the weaker his body became—and challenged my own faith. I pray his faith will challenge yours as well.

Heavenly Father,

Forgive me for taking life for granted, for being consumed with things that are not eternally important. Teach me to number my days that I might live each day for You. Amen.

For the rest of your life . . .

live each day—each moment—as if it were your last on this earth.

135

66

THE GOAL
OF PERFECTION

*Not that I have already obtained all this, or
have already been made perfect . . .*
PHILIPPIANS 3:12

*I*t's human nature at all ages to strive to be the best. Little kids try to win footraces; teens want to look their best or be the smartest; men aim to end up in the corner office; moms seek the best for their children and their varied endeavors.

How do we tell the difference between the God-given desire for excellence and the often self-serving attempt to be number one? Where is the line, and how do you know when you've crossed it? I've learned to tell this way: when what I *do* has a negative impact on who I *am* in Christ.

In the best sense of the word, I think the apostle Paul must have been a perfectionist. (Perfectionism isn't a sin. If I were having brain surgery, I would want my doctor to be a perfectionist!) And yet Paul made it clear that being the best at anything without also being Christlike was pure vanity: "If I have a faith that can move mountains, but have not love, I am nothing. If I give all I possess to the poor and surrender my body to the flames, but have not love, I gain nothing" (1 Cor. 13:2–3). I believe Paul was saying that who we are in Christ is *more important* than what we do for Christ.

But what if we strive to be "the most loving" Christian around? Even in the holy pursuit of love, there can be a snare if we pursue it with tainted motives. God doesn't want us to become our own trophies, displaying our own abilities. He wants us to become trophies of His grace, revealing to the world that the work He does in and through us is of far more value than the work we do on our own. Instead of our trying to be humanly perfect (an impossible task), we can reveal His perfect character as we allow Christ to live His life in us (see Gal. 2:20).

Ultimately our pursuit of excellence is about attracting others to the original, and ultimate, source of excellence, God Himself.

Heavenly Father,

Forgive me for the times when I have sought to be the best for my sake instead of for Yours. Help me pursue divine excellence, not human perfection. Amen.

———— *For the rest of your life . . .* ————

live in a way that reveals how excellent He is and His ways are.

67

RISING ABOVE REJECTION

Am I now trying to win the approval of men, or of God?
Or am I trying to please men? If I were still trying to
please men, I would not be a servant of Christ.
GALATIANS 1:10

Many of us suffer from a disease called people-pleasing. We believe that as long as others are happy with us, God must be happy with us too. Even going back to our childhood, we remember the pain of rejection. It's often not until we make up our mind to follow Christ, no matter what age that is, that the Holy Spirit begins to deal with our heart concerning this overrated fear.

Jesus was rejected by many of the people who met Him. If we follow Him, we can expect the same reaction. If they persecuted Jesus, they will persecute us as well. As long as we fear the rejection of others, we will not be able to walk in true freedom in Christ or to obey Him without reserve.

Maybe the rejection you experience is not because you are a Christian. Maybe it's simply not having enough in common with others, or the way you look or act, or something you did. Jesus experienced this as well. People thought he was boasting about his relationship with God. They did not believe His miracles.

They mocked where He came from. He was completely misunderstood in what He said and did. But Christ did not let others' opinions affect who He knew He was.

Our God, who is the King of kings and the Ruler of the universe, has already proclaimed that you are accepted in Christ. You have been chosen, redeemed, forgiven, loved, adopted, justified, secured, and completed in Christ. Even when you make mistakes you are not condemned, but fully restored by God through your repentant heart.

If people reject you for any reason, turn to the only One whose acceptance really matters. He will take care of those who have misjudged you and give you the courage to say, "Lord, forgive them, for they know not what they do."

Though forgiveness may seem out of the question, with Christ all things are possible. The rejection you experience now may hurt at the moment, but in time Christ will restore your heart and bless your faithfulness. Ultimately, would you rather be exalted by men or by God? I think I know your answer.

Heavenly Father,

Thank You that in Your sight I will never be rejected, that I have been accepted now and forever. If I am rejected by others, help me to love them the way You love me. Amen.

For the rest of your life . . .

let rejection on earth for Christ's sake remind you of your acceptance in heaven.

68

TRUE JOY

Jesus, full of joy through the Holy Spirit . . .
LUKE 10:21

*M*artin Luther was the German monk who ignited the Protestant Reformation in 1517. He lived in despair of ever finding peace with God until he understood God's grace and forgiveness. Even after becoming a Christian, it would be easy to think of him as a pious, celibate, and sober theologian. But such was not the case.

Luther married, had children, and made his home a gathering place for young theology students. He loved to laugh, tell stories, and spend hours around the table reveling in the joy he had discovered in Christ. Martin Luther was not only a model of theological faithfulness; he was also an example of the joy of the Spirit.

Sadly, too many people think that the price one pays for becoming a Christian is to give up any idea of fun or joy or laughter. They have heard that the mark of a Christian is not to "smoke, drink, or chew, or hang out with people who do." While the four Gospels in the New Testament do not tell us about Jesus' humor, we do read in Luke 10:21 that He was "full of joy through the Holy Spirit." He had sent the young disciples out on a ministry trip, and when they returned with joy (10:17), He was full of joy as well. I can just see Jesus entering into the excitement they expressed as they told Him what had happened on their ministry trip.

But what is true joy? It is not necessarily laughter or happiness. It actually goes much deeper. Paul wrote his "epistle of joy" to the Philippians while in prison in Rome. So joy is obviously not based on circumstances.

True joy comes from the fullness of the Holy Spirit (see Gal. 5:18, 22) and results when we recognize that we are completely accepted in Christ—that no circumstance or trial or failure on our part can alter our standing with God.

That's what Martin Luther lacked before he experienced the fullness of the Holy Spirit, and that's why he was full of joy afterward. It's why we should be full of joy as well.

Heavenly Father,

Thank You for teaching me that there is more joy and genuine laughter in Your kingdom than in this world. Help me to rejoice— to enjoy the abundant life Jesus gives. Amen.

For the rest of your life . . .

experience true joy knowing that nothing can separate you from the love of God in Christ Jesus.

6 9

LETTING GO

*"Do not let your hearts be troubled.
Trust in God; trust also in me."*

JOHN 14:1

Good-byes are always painful. For children it's the letting
go of comfort, love, and security—like when parents drop
their little ones off at the church nursery. The parents are still
right there, watching through the one-way window; but because
their toddler can't see them, he thinks they've gone forever and
lets everyone know how unhappy he is at this sudden turn of
events.

Babies aren't the only ones who experience the pain and
fear of good-byes. We fear we won't see that friend or loved one
again—that something will separate us forever. Fear is nothing
more than walking by sight, not by faith, regarding the future
(see 2 Cor. 5:7).

Jesus said good-bye to His disciples more than once, trying to get them to understand that He would be returning to
heaven from whence He had come. They obviously were fearful
about this reality because Jesus comforted them and tried to
assure them that He would return, uniting them again (see John
14:1–14). Not only did Jesus comfort them with His promises;

He sent the Comforter, the Holy Spirit, to live in them in His absence. And after He ascended to heaven and sent the disciples out to spread the gospel, "the Lord worked with them" as they went (Mark 16:20).

Do we really live as though Christ is with us? Circumstances may make us feel alone. Those around us may seem distant. Has God totally abandoned us? Like toddlers we look through the window of life and fail to see Christ standing on the other side. He's been there all along, watching and caring about everything that concerns us (see 1 Pet. 5:7).

The presence of the Holy Spirit means that Christ has never really left us at all! Granted, He is not on this earth physically, but spiritually He is in our hearts (see Gal. 2:20). After all, has not God said, "Never will I leave you; never will I forsake you" (Heb. 13:5)? Don't allow your eyes to deceive your heart. As far as Christ is concerned, you will never be alone.

Heavenly Father,

How glad I am that one day Jesus will return for His church! And how thankful I am that He lives in me spiritually; that He will never leave or forsake me. Amen.

For the rest of your life . . .

learn to trust God with the future—
yours and your children's.

143

FILLED WITH THE SPIRIT

Do not get drunk on wine, which leads to debauchery.
Instead, be filled with the Spirit.
EPHESIANS 5:18

We're aware of what happens when someone is under the influence of too much alcohol. That person's ability to control his faculties is given over to another power. This may be part of the reason Paul used that illustration in talking about being filled with the Spirit: when we're filled with the Spirit, we are under His influence and control.

When we come to believe in Christ as our Savior, the Holy Spirit enters our lives to guide, direct, comfort, and empower us. But being filled with the Spirit does not mean we should anticipate some special feeling, for it is a matter of faith. Nor is the filling of the Spirit a one-time event; it's a process. And it doesn't mean we are free from sin—though we should anticipate new power over the sins of the flesh.

Since our lives are a vessel through which Christ ministers, they must be kept pure. Therefore we remain filled with the Spirit by confessing all known sin (see 1 John 1:9), yielding to His direction (see Ps. 119:133), and trusting God to be at work in our lives (see Prov. 3:5–6). The more we yield each area of our lives to the Spirit, and learn to surrender to Him daily, the more we walk by faith and are filled with the Spirit.

In Billy Graham's book *The Holy Spirit*, he described the daily filling of the Spirit: "I find it helpful to begin each day by submitting that day into God's hands. . . . I ask Him to take my life that day and use it for His glory. I ask Him to cleanse me from anything that would hinder His work in my life. And then I step out in faith knowing that the Holy Spirit is filling me continually as I trust in Him and obey His Word. Sometimes during the day I may not be aware of His presence and sometimes I am. But at the end of the day I can look back and thank Him because I see His hand at work. He promised to be with me that day and He has been!"

I want to be under the influence—but only the influence of the Holy Spirit. By yielding our lives to Him we will experience the joy of intimacy with Christ.

Heavenly Father,

I want to submit all of my life to You. Forgive me for trying to take back control of my life. Fill me with Your Spirit today and every day. Amen.

———— *For the rest of your life . . .* ————

drink daily from the cup of Christ
so that you may be full of His Spirit.

145

PATIENCE
THROUGH SUFFERING

Consider it pure joy, my brothers, whenever
you face trials of many kinds.
JAMES 1:2

Oswald Chambers defined patience as more than endurance: "A saint's life is in the hands of God like a bow and arrow in the hands of an archer. God is aiming at something the saint cannot see and He stretches and strains the saint. Often the saint thinks he cannot take anymore. Then God continues to stretch until His purpose is in sight and then He lets us fly." In other words, when we think God is not coming to our rescue, He is in fact performing an even greater miracle than merely changing our circumstances to make us more comfortable. Instead He is changing us within.

The apostle James tells us what the testing of our faith produces: perseverance leading to maturity and completeness of faith (see James 1:3). And the apostle Paul said that "our present sufferings are not worth comparing with the glory that will be revealed in us" (Rom. 8:18). He also said that God causes all things, including our sufferings, to work together for good to those who love God (see v. 28). Our experiences of suffering have a purpose beyond what we can see from our limited perspective.

How do we learn to view all of life's difficulties from God's perspective? By the renewing of our mind; by reading daily the promises of God's Word, which tells us what is true . . . tells us how to think . . . tells us what to do when we suffer: "Cast all your anxiety on him because he cares for you" (1 Pet. 5:7). Our Heavenly Father is perfectly trustworthy, and He alone knows exactly what each of us must endure in order to have proven character formed in us.

God's purpose in creating us is to have a relationship with us and enjoy our fellowship. How much of our attention would God get if our lives were always rosy? Our chief purpose in life is to bring glory to God. One of the greatest ways to glorify God is to maintain our hope and trust in Him when the trials of life would lead us to do otherwise.

Heavenly Father,

I have suffered in the past, and I know I will suffer in the future. I want to learn to suffer with patience and faith, trusting that Your purposes for my life are being accomplished. Amen.

——————— *For the rest of your life . . .* ———————

let trials be the stones that pave your way to the kingdom of God.

WAITING ON GOD

*But those who hope in the LORD will renew their
strength. They will soar on wings like eagles; they will
run and not grow weary, they will walk and not be faint.*

ISAIAH 40:31

Is there anyone today who doesn't feel pulled in a thousand different directions? Whether you are married or not, a mother or not, employed or not . . . if you are alive in the twenty-first century, you are likely very busy.

My constant prayer for years has been, "Lord, please prioritize my day." Without the confidence that God is answering that prayer on a moment-by-moment basis, I would have no confidence about the order of my day. Praying is a way of waiting on God. It puts Him and His agenda ahead of me and mine. Without pausing to wait on God, I would charge into the day unequipped, unprotected, and unprepared for the demands that lay ahead.

No one could possibly have felt the pressure of demands more than Jesus. Yet we get a picture of Him from Scripture of never being overwhelmed. He always seemed to know when it was time to come or go, speak or listen, act or be still. He never let those who needed Him get in the way of His need for God.

In fact, He was willing to walk away from crowds of needy people to spend time waiting on God if He felt the need to do so.

Drawing apart from this world to spend time waiting on God requires intentional choices on our part. It means finding our ultimate affirmation from God instead of from family and friends. It means finding our esteem in the presence of God rather than in how many things are on our calendar or to-do list. Waiting on God in His presence can cause us to change our plans, to stop succumbing to the demands of a hurried world.

When we wait on God, we are ready to be directed. Our attention is on Him, and we aren't distracted by the noise and news of this world. Our problems, challenges, and agendas look different when viewed against the backdrop of His calming presence. Making God our priority somehow prioritizes everything else.

Heavenly Father,

I am tired of finding myself overwhelmed by life's demands—too much to do and too little time to do it. By Your grace I am going to wait upon You to give me the plans for my day. Amen.

For the rest of your life . . .

*use times of waiting on God
to refocus your priorities for God.*

73

FINANCIAL SECURITY

"Do not worry about your life, what you will eat; or
about your body, what you will wear. . . . But seek his
kingdom, and these things will be given to you as well."

LUKE 12:22, 31

We live in a world consumed with gaining material advantage. We monitor newspapers, television, and the Internet to see how the financial market is doing. Many people keep one eye on live news feeds from the markets all day on television or the Internet. Sometimes you can actually see peoples' moods fluctuate according to how the stock market is doing. If we have a little, we want it to become a lot; and if we have a lot, we are worried it will become a little.

Trusting in money or possessions to provide for our peace of mind is a poor investment. No matter how much money we have, we never seem to have enough. It was John D. Rockefeller who, when asked, "How much money is enough?" replied, "Just a little bit more."

Nevertheless, many people trust money to make them feel safe and provide a sense of fulfillment. And what do you get in return? Worry and stress. William H. Vanderbilt said, "The care of hundreds of millions is enough to kill anyone. There is no pleasure in it." The more you have, the more you have to decide what to do with it or how to preserve it. Then, just like the stock market, those feelings of false security come crashing down when you least expect them to.

Jesus said, "You cannot serve both God and Money" (Matt. 6:24). In essence He was saying we need to seek either an earthly kingdom or God's kingdom. But we are deceiving ourselves to think that we can seek after both.

Jesus did not say it was wrong to make money or to live in a nice home. But He did say not to seek those things as an end in themselves. Instead we are to seek God's kingdom first, after which God will add to our lives that which we need to live on (see Matt. 6:33). Whatever God supplies, make sure it all remains "His," not "mine," when it comes to ultimate ownership.

Investing with God will produce returns that He will stand behind for eternity.

Heavenly Father,

I know that everything I have comes from You. Help me to be a good steward and build up treasure in heaven instead of on earth. Amen.

———————— *For the rest of your life . . .* ————————

practice on earth what you will find in heaven—
which doesn't include the love of money.

74

THE CROWN
OF PERSEVERANCE

*Blessed is the man who perseveres under trial, because
when he has stood the test, he will receive the crown of
life that God has promised to those who love him.*

JAMES 1:12

Susanna Wesley is at the top of my list of nominees for the
"Mother-Wife-Saint" award. The wife of a preacher in
England at the turn of the eighteenth century, Susanna bore
nineteen children, nine of whom died. Two of these children,
John and Charles, became the early leaders of the Methodist
movement and were mightily used by God.

Throughout her life, Susanna endured every trial a woman
could imagine: financial ruin, a husband who left her, and many
children who died. Yet trials seemed to cause her spiritual roots
to grow ever deeper in Christ. She trained all her children in the
nurture and admonition of the Lord. Tradition has it that, to
maintain her own daily "quiet time" in a small house filled with
children, she would sit in a chair and cover her head with her
voluminous skirt to block out distractions, warning her children
not to disturb her. Just before she died, her husband returned

and wrote a letter to their children saying they owed all that they were to their mother.

Perhaps a loved one has abandoned you. Perhaps you are a widow carrying the load of child rearing by yourself. Perhaps you are poor by this world's standards. Perhaps you have no time or place to call your own. If so, you are not alone. You are like every believer who is called to persevere . . . and for whom a crown is reserved if you will but remain faithful. On the days that you wonder how you will make it, remember that God is with you, asking for your trust.

Perseverance is a daily commitment, a daily relinquishing of the world's idea that life is supposed to go our way. It is a daily confession that we are willing for life to go God's way instead of ours. It is a daily agreement that God is with us in heartbreak, poverty, or aloneness. It is a daily affirmation that we can do all things through Christ who strengthens us (see Phil. 4:13). If you make that commitment . . . confession . . . agreement . . . affirmation, you will persevere no matter what . . . and one day receive your own "crown of life."

Heavenly Father,

Grant me the perseverance of a Susanna Wesley. Let me learn to trust You in difficult times and have the discipline to seek You daily. May my children see You as their refuge as well. Amen.

For the rest of your life . . .

prove your perseverance by staying the course in spite of every inclination to turn aside.

75

COMPLETE SURRENDER

"Anyone who comes to me but refuses to let go of father,
mother, spouse, children, brothers, sisters—yes, even
one's own self!—can't be my disciple."
LUKE 14:26 *THE MESSAGE*

When we become Christians, we have great expectations about what we want to achieve in our new spiritual life: new friends, new reputation, new strength to overcome old habits, and maybe a new ministry. We have plans for what we want to do for God and decide we'll bring Him along. But the biblical concept of "surrender to Christ" is not part of our thinking. At least it wasn't part of mine.

In battles and wars, it's always the losers who surrender. And we don't want to think of ourselves as losers. Nor do we want to think of having to give up anything to God: "I surrender all . . ." as the hymn says, is not an enticing thought.

But if we're honest, we'll realize that we are losers—failures at this thing called life: "For all have sinned and fall short of the glory of God" (Rom. 3:23). We eat too much, drink too much, talk too much, criticize too much, spend too much, envy too much, and worry too much. It takes a measured amount of delusion to say that "Everything's just great!" when we know it isn't.

That's why we need to surrender to Jesus Christ and be His disciple. Jesus lived life and won, even conquering death in the process. And He invites us to follow Him and partake of His victory—the abundant life we were created to experience but have failed at on our own.

And He also invites us to trust Him with the parts of life that are way too much for us to handle: terminal illness, divorce, financial crises, wayward children. Jesus is not put off by any of these desperate circumstances and invites us to give them (surrender them) to Him.

The irony in surrender is that it takes more strength to lose than to win. But even that strength comes from Christ. So don't be afraid to sing "I surrender all" and mean it. There's true wisdom in giving up what's broken to the only Person who can fix it.

Heavenly Father,

Thank You for being someone to whom I want to surrender. Please help me see the parts of my life I am still clinging to as my own. Amen.

For the rest of your life . . .

surrender to God every part of your life on a daily basis.

76

WHO DO YOU
THINK YOU ARE?

Faith comes by hearing, and hearing by the word of God.
ROMANS 10:17 NKJV

*I*t has been said that we are not who we think we are, nor are we who other people think we are. Instead we are who we think other people think we are. If that sounds confusing, it boils down to this: the mind is a powerful instrument just waiting to be told what to believe.

We see this worked out in the lives of children; they will believe anything! That is both a blessing and a danger. Some who live in an environment of unconditional love overflow with exuberance and a passion for life. They think they are OK because those they are around have told them they are. Others, whose surroundings have been more conditional, approach life with a fear of failing. They hold back, listening to internal tapes that say they're not OK. They don't know why; they just have a nagging suspicion that they're missing something important.

Our mind is constantly learning what to think. If we have no gatekeeper, then any piece of information, true or false, can wander in and take up residence (see 2 Pet. 2:1–3).

But if our mind is guarded by a filter that rejects error and only allows truth to come in, we learn to think correctly about ourselves, others, and the world we live in. Jesus said that the truth will make us free and that it is Satan who speaks lies as his native language (see John 8:32, 44). We can learn to think by default (believing whatever the world and others tell us) or by discipline (believing what God says about life and about ourselves). We can believe that powerful, pretty, prominent, and prosperous is the goal; or we can believe that God's values—loving, faithful, loyal, humble, and servant hearted—are the goal. The filter, of course, is the Bible, where we learn what God thinks.

Forget what you think and what others think. Find out what God thinks about you. Reading His Word is the only way to learn who you really are.

Heavenly Father,

Keep me from listening to the world and its lies, and help me discipline myself to renew my mind with Your truth. Amen.

— For the rest of your life . . . —

remember maturity in life is a function of receiving and applying truth about life.

77

BELIEVE IT OR NOT

"Everything is possible for him who believes."
MARK 9:23

A father brought his demon-possessed son to Christ and said, "If you can do anything, take pity on us and help us." Jesus rebuked the man by saying, "'*If* you can'? . . . Everything is possible for him who believes." And the man cried out, "I do believe; help me overcome my unbelief" (Mark 9:22–24). Then Jesus healed the man's son. In essence, Jesus was saying to the man, "The problem is not My power but your faith."

We can all relate to the desperate feelings of the father in this story. Intellectually we know that God loves us. He demonstrated that love through the death of His Son on the cross. But emotionally our hearts, when broken, can overpower our heads. If things don't go our way, or we find ourselves in a hopeless situation, we become confused and begin to doubt that which we thought we understood—that God is faithful. We pout. We stop praying. And we stop fellowshipping with other believers or going to church. It's our way of getting back at God for His inability to respond to our need.

But as Christ told the father, the problem is not with God's ability but our faith. When we find ourselves pulling away from

God, we must cry out like the father: "Help me overcome my unbelief. Give me greater faith and patience and endurance. Help me to keep my eyes on You until this situation is resolved in one way or another. I know that nothing is impossible for You, and everything is possible for the one who believes. And I believe, Lord!" Faith is only increased as we move toward the object of our faith, Jesus Christ. Not only can Jesus meet your need and come to the rescue, but He wants to increase your faith in the process.

Whatever the circumstance or no matter how far you have gone astray, God wants to give you greater faith—believe it or not.

Heavenly Father,

Forgive me for not trusting that You can and will meet my every need. Help me to remember that my faith in You is all that matters. Amen.

——— For the rest of your life . . . ———

*increase your faith by choosing to believe
that God can act on your behalf.*

78

Transformed by Truth

Do not conform any longer to the pattern of this world,
but be transformed by the renewing of your mind.
ROMANS 12:2

It's not taught in any class in high school or college, but cramming is a skill most students learn to acquire. Those late-night sessions where we tried to internalize a semester's worth of information in a matter of hours are a rite of passage for all students. And, in fact, cramming often works when an exam the next morning is the goal. The question is, of course, how much of that information becomes part of your life? How much can you recall a week after the test?

The goal of study in the spiritual life is not information but transformation. Yes, there are tests in the Christian life—and that makes my point: we never know when the tests will occur, so we have to be ready all the time. That is, we have to have the information about how to pass life's tests available and usable every day. Tests in the Christian life are like the pop quizzes we used to have in high school or college. The idea is to stay "studied up" on the class content day by day so that, should a test be announced, we are prepared.

How would you advise a student to stay prepared for pop quizzes during the semester? You'd tell him or her to set aside some time every day to review the material from that day's class and previous classes. Reviewing every day gradually transforms one's thinking about math, science, economics—whatever the subject matter might be.

Consider your daily quiet time in the same way—a time to review new and old material on a daily basis. Staying current with God's information on forgiveness, love, self-control, witnessing, the family—whatever the subject matter—keeps us ready for the unannounced quizzes that come our way.

Is your goal in life Christian information or spiritual transformation? If the latter, then do the only thing that will transform your thinking: review the Word of God daily, prayerfully asking God to allow it to renew your mind. It's the only way to pass the tests and move on to the next level as a different person.

Heavenly Father,

I want so much to be more like You. Help me to take the long view on what I am learning, to value transformation more than information. Amen.

—————— For the rest of your life . . . ——————

study Scripture like you want to, not like you have to.

161

79

PRINCIPLES OF PRAYER

One day Jesus was praying in a certain place. When he finished, one of his disciples said to him, "Lord, teach us to pray, just as John taught his disciples."

LUKE 11:1

There is a story of two unfortunate men in the Old Testament, Nadab and Abihu. They took it upon themselves to play the role of priests and to offer unauthorized fire and incense before the Lord, and they died as a result of their actions (see Lev. 10:1–7). Some might think God's actions were harsh, that He ought to be thankful people would approach Him at all. Apparently that's not the case.

There are principles, ways of doing things, in every area of life. And there were principles in the Old Testament by which priests and worshippers were to approach God—principles of holiness. While we don't offer fiery sacrifices before God today, there are principles for how we should draw near to Him in prayer. These are not life-or-death principles but guidelines—ways to pray, which the Bible reveals, that will make our communication with the holy God of the universe pleasing to Him and beneficial to us.

"Can't we just talk to Him?" you ask. Yes, but think of it this way: the Queen of England is a person to whom we can "just talk," but she is also a reigning monarch. Protocols in place preserve the majesty of her office and establish the proper footing for communication. It's the same with God. Talking with God is not like talking over the back fence with a buddy. We may speak English in both cases, but we speak it differently.

Here are nine principles to keep in mind: when you pray, pray in the Spirit (see John 4:23), expectantly (see Matt. 7:8), specifically (see Mark 10:51), patiently (see Heb. 6:12), in His will (see 1 John 5:14), in faith (see Mark 11:22–24), with thanksgiving (see Phil. 1:3–4), often (see 1 Thess. 5:17), and with boldness (see Luke 11:5–10). These are not nine slots that, when filled with prayer-coins, will dispense an answer. Think of them as reflecting the character of God, ways to talk to God that He appreciates. Because these principles are biblical, we know they are true. Keep them in mind as you pray.

Heavenly Father,

Thank You for inviting me to talk with You. Please teach me to pray in a way that honors who You are and that deepens my relationship with You. Amen.

For the rest of your life . . .

make prayer better in your life by faithful practice and following God's principles.

163

THE TREASURE
OF YOUR HEART

*"For where your treasure is, there your
heart will be also."*
LUKE 12:34

What is most important to you in life? What is the one thing you could not live without? Your family? Your health? Your money? Your reputation? The answer is what the Bible calls your treasure.

There are times in my life when my heart is filled with love and joy for Jesus and He is all I want. And yet there are other times when I let the world persuade me that other things are more important. That realization makes me painfully aware of my humanity, my fleshly human nature. It makes me know how much I must continually choose to make Christ and His kingdom the true treasure of my life. Words, choices, thoughts, actions, decisions, purchases—all become a trail of evidence about what is important to me. Do you consider Christ a treasure in your life right now? How do you know?

Oftentimes we claim that Christ is our treasure, and yet our life demonstrates otherwise. We say we want to please God but worry so much more about pleasing others. We hesitate to talk about our relationship with Christ but easily discuss our relationships with friends. We are reluctant when asked to give money to the church but jump quickly to purchase the latest designer clothes.

It's important to take a good look at your life because your actions often reflect where your true heart is. How you live speaks louder than what you say. Where do you spend most of your time or money? What do you most enjoy doing? Are you task oriented or people oriented? Take inventory. Look at your calendar, your checkbook, and your phone calls. Notice what is important in your life, for those are your treasures. Tell Jesus today and every day that you want Him to be your treasure—that you want to center your life around Him. In time you will sense a difference, for your life will reflect your love for Him, and there will be no question where your heart is.

Heavenly Father,

Forgive me for sometimes having my heart in heaven and sometimes in this world. May my heart be wholly Yours so my life will make a difference. Amen.

——— For the rest of your life . . . ———

set your heart in God's direction by first investing your treasure in heaven.

165

81

NOURISHING YOUR SOUL

"I am the bread of life."
JOHN 6:48

No one likes to be hungry; we get irritated and feel desperate to fill the emptiness inside. The same is true spiritually. Just as our stomachs ache when not filled with food, so our heart and soul ache when not filled with God. God has put eternity in our hearts (see Eccles. 3:11)—a longing for God—and to fill the heart with anything else is to leave it malnourished. You can be sure that your spiritual soul is hungry for God if it's been awhile since your last spiritual meal. You may have noticed the symptoms: less patience, kindness, and love toward others. These are the hunger pangs of an empty heart.

All the attributes that demonstrate the presence of the Holy Spirit begin to dissipate unless we are nourished by the only One who can satisfy. The more we have been satisfied with the nourishment of God's love, His Word, and His presence, the more we will yearn for it when it is missing. But there is a subtle danger: with enough time away, we may not realize that we are even hungry at all. We might begin to feed on the things of this world that provide only temporary satisfaction, oblivious to the spiritual-nutritional crisis that is coming. We forget that we were created for fellowship with the Father, to love Him and be loved by Him. He, and He alone, is our daily bread. St. Augustine said, "Our hearts are restless until they find their rest in Thee."

Jesus said, "I am the bread of life. . . . If anyone eats of this bread, he will live forever" (John 6:48, 51). To eat the bread of life means to accept Christ into our lives as Savior and to become united with Him. We are united with Him as we study His Word daily, commune with Him through prayer, and live lives of obedience.

To feed our stomachs is a temporary pleasure, but to feed our souls with the bread of life is a pleasure that satisfies now and forever.

Heavenly Father,

Help me to consume Your will and Your Word as the sustenance of my life. Show me how little the world has to offer that will truly sustain my soul. Amen.

For the rest of your life . . .

avoid spiritual malnourishment by feeding on the bread from heaven.

167

SECRET OF SUBMISSION

Submit to one another out of reverence for Christ.
EPHESIANS 5:21

The word *submission* is often associated with weakness or the devaluing of one's position, but it's actually just the opposite. To be submissive does not mean to be walked on. It means to have the opportunity to lift others up, to respect or to honor others. In fact, Christ calls both men and women to submit to each other (see Eph. 5:21); to serve and subject ourselves to one another; to move further away from selfishness; and in this way, to begin to reflect His character.

Putting someone above yourself requires wisdom, patience, courage, and humility; it requires strength of character. If Christ, the King of kings, can submit to His role as a servant on this earth, giving up His rightful position of authority, how much more should we willingly take His same attitude (see Phil. 2:5). This is the secret of submission: it is an honor to submit, not a humiliation. In fact, 1 Peter 3:1 says the best way a wife can win her husband to the Lord is not by her words but by her act of love and submission. This is true of everyone with whom we come in contact. That's why the Scriptures teach us to place others' interests ahead of our own (see Phil. 2:3).

Whether we are called to submit to a husband, an employer, a committee chairperson, or a government official, the principle is the same: if we are submitted to Christ, we will not chafe at the idea of submitting to others. Conversely, if submitting to others is difficult, it may be because we are not wholly submitted to Christ.

The headship of another person does not mean that we cannot give input or ask questions (or even refuse if our submission causes disobedience to God). However, it does mean that the leader is the one ultimately accountable to God for the leadership decisions, and we are accountable to God for how we submit to his or her leadership.

Whether you are a leader or a follower, we all submit to God, the Ultimate Authority.

Heavenly Father,

I know submission is not a value to be learned in this world. Help me to live out the values of Your kingdom and be willing to submit whenever I'm asked. Amen.

————— *For the rest of your life . . .* —————

*glorify God by finding honor in the call
to submit to another person.*

83

BEING STILL

"Be still, and know that I am God."
PSALM 46:10

We live in an overscheduled society. Most of us spend time, even on the weekends, doing things we *have* to do instead of doing things we *want* to do. We have become so used to a hurried and frazzled existence that we are oblivious to the growing physical and emotional stress we put on ourselves. With the combination of cable television, Internet, faxes, and cell phones, the opportunities for interruptions are endless.

God will not stand in line with all the others who want our attention. Without making a conscious choice to get away and be alone with God, we would just keep moving on, all the while believing that busyness is the way to a productive day.

God said, "Be still, and know that I am God." Yet our world thinks if you are still, you are not accomplishing anything. Something is wrong with your life, or you must be lazy and incompetent in some way if you are not moving at full speed. But stillness can be powerful and productive.

Have you ever noticed what it's like when a speaker is talking and suddenly pauses or when an orchestra plays and there is a moment of silence? Much like the calm after a storm, the quietness can be profound.

But it's often in the middle of a crisis that you cannot hear God. In the midst of all the noise—banging on His door or crying out for a response—He might wait before He speaks. There must be a stillness born out of trust. For that is when God tends to speak.

Maybe that's why Elijah heard God after all the noise had faded. Maybe God knew Elijah would hear him better in a gentle whisper (see 1 Kings 19:12) than during all the winds and fire and earthquakes. Even Jesus got away often to be still, knowing that only then could He hear clearly from the Father.

Since we are all so used to scheduling, let's schedule time to be still—to be alone with God. You may find that the quieter your surroundings, the louder His voice becomes.

Heavenly Father,

Keep me from being so busy. Help me to find daily time alone with You to be still and listen to what You would have me know. Amen.

—————— *For the rest of your life . . .* ——————

turn down the volume of the world and listen
for the whisper of God.

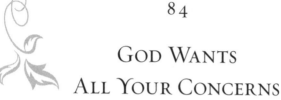

84

GOD WANTS
ALL YOUR CONCERNS

Cast all your anxiety on him because he cares for you.
1 PETER 5:7

A stumbling block for many Christians who want to turn their worries over to God is the fear of becoming a nuisance. We sometimes think, *I hate to bother God with all my concerns. I'm sure He has much bigger things to take care of.* Or if we don't fear being a nuisance, we think we are too small in God's eyes for Him to direct attention to our need.

Think of the universe as a giant radar screen, and that concern makes sense. You and I would barely show up as a blip on such a gigantic backdrop. But that is from our perspective, not God's. The Bible tells us that God sees sparrows and knows the number of hairs on our head (see Luke 12:6–7). Those illustrations Jesus used let us know that if God sees our hairs, He certainly sees us.

Just imagine you overheard your child telling her friend that she couldn't bring a problem to you because you had more important things to think about. Would you not be heartbroken? I can't imagine a parent who wouldn't. It's no different with

God. He loves each of us as His precious children and tells us to give Him every concern we have (see 1 Pet. 5:7). He reminds us that He is involved in every detail of our lives (see Ps. 139:1–7). He knew us before we were born (see Jer. 1:5), knows all about us (see Matt. 10:30), and has a special plan for our lives (see Jer. 29:11). His desire is for us to love Him with all our heart (see Matt. 22:37) and turn to Him with every trial we face so He can direct our paths (see Prov. 3:6).

Next time you are hesitant to share with God what is going on in your life, just remember, God does not use a grid to screen our concerns, hearing only the major ones. Instead He uses a funnel with a wide mouth into which we can pour all our concerns—major, minor, and in between. God is the only one in the world who wants to hear all your concerns.

Heavenly Father,

Thank You for caring about every concern that I have, whether large or small. May I learn to come before Your throne with innocence and boldness, as a child approaches her father in times of need. Amen.

For the rest of your life . . .

remember God has nothing more important in the universe to attend to than you.

85

BELIEVING GOD

Now faith is being sure of what we hope for
and certain of what we do not see.

HEBREWS 11:1

Sometimes when young Christians hear the phrase "believe God," they do a double take. Do you mean, believe *in* God? they think. No, they heard correctly: "Believe God." Young Christians have just exercised faith *in* God, and it takes some maturing for them to learn that "believing God" is the heart of the Christian walk.

Believing God shouldn't sound that strange to us. When trusted friends tell us something "unbelievable," we say, "I believe you!" By that we mean we have confidence in them, don't doubt them, believe they are speaking the truth. And that's exactly what it means to "believe God." It means we have confidence that what He has promised He will bring to pass.

Here's a helpful way to think about belief: non-Christians learn to believe *in* God for their salvation whereas Christians believe God for their sanctification. Any Christian who wants to have real faith for a real world must be a Christian who believes God.

Hebrews 11:1 says that faith is being sure (not doubting) of what we hope for and certain (again, not doubting) of what we do not see. This definition retranslates "hope" from a pace-the-floor kind of hope to a sleep-like-a-baby anticipation. It is faith that gives assurance to hope. If we are certain of what we do not see (certain God is going to provide something that hasn't yet materialized), we are the people Paul described in 2 Corinthians 5:7—those who walk by faith, not by sight.

If you have believed in God through His Son, Jesus Christ, you then need to become a person who believes God, who takes Him at His Word; who does not doubt Him, who walks on the basis of His promises instead of what can be seen with the eyes. We live in a deceitful world where things are often not as they appear. That's why walking by sight is dangerous, not to mention shortsighted.

If you tell a good friend, "I believe you," how much more should you tell God the same thing?

Heavenly Father,

I want to believe You; help me when my faith is weak. Grant me faith to live with confidence in Your promises. Amen.

—————— *For the rest of your life . . .* ——————

make it a practice to memorize Scripture so you will never be without reasons to believe God.

175

86

CONFESSION COUNTS

*Therefore confess your sins to each other and pray for
each other so that you may be healed. The prayer of a
righteous man is powerful and effective.*
JAMES 5:16

*I*f you want to have power in your prayer life, you must regularly confess your sins. God wants to remove anything that
would separate you from Him and you from others.

How often have we simply prayed, "Lord, forgive me for all
my sins" without making a conscious effort to discover our faults
or shortcomings? More than our words, God wants our hearts;
He wants to see a changed life. Real confession springs from
a repentant heart, and a repentant heart follows through with
a change of behavior. What about when we have offended, or been
offended by, another person? Pride keeps the offense concealed.
But real confession (that which desires to please God) follows
through and seeks reconciliation (confession and/or forgiveness,
as required) from that person. The person who, above everything
else, desires a real and loving relationship with God will have
a real and loving relationship with others (see Col. 3:13).

In Psalm 139:23–24, David shows what it means to *want*
to confess his sins to God: "Search me, O God, and know my

heart; test me and know my anxious thoughts. See if there is any offensive way in me, and lead me in the way everlasting." He apparently had confessed everything he knew about, so he went a step beyond; he asked God to search his heart and see if there was anything else that was an offense and needed to be confessed. Surely that is the spirit of confession God is looking for in us.

The promise of God is that "if we confess our sins, he is faithful and just and will forgive us our sins and purify us from all unrighteousness" (1 John 1:9). In other words, there is a purpose for forgiveness: to be cleansed from the effects of sin in our life. If we don't confess our unrighteousness, it remains as a barrier between God and us.

After all, it is the prayer of a *righteous* man that accomplishes much, James wrote. Is timely confession of sin a missing ingredient in your prayer life? Ask God to search your heart today, and be prepared to confess whatever He reveals.

Heavenly Father,

I confess that confession is hard. Please give me the humility to bare my soul, to admit that I have sinned, to find reconciliation with You and others. Amen.

--------- *For the rest of your life . . .* ---------

confess any sin, reconcile any offense,
the moment you become aware of it.

87

GLORIFYING GOD

"Call upon me in the day of trouble; I will
deliver you, and you will honor me."
PSALM 50:15

o you know what it means to bring glory to God? It is letting others see who God is by seeing who you are—a person
who honors God by calling upon (depending on) Him. Are you
self-sufficient or God-sufficient?

Living a life that glorifies God is synonymous with living a
life that reveals who God is—One who is worthy of our trust and
dependence. There are many in this world who may not read the
Bible, but they will read our lives. As Paul suggested, Christians
are letters to be read by all (see 2 Cor. 3:2–3).

Turning to God in times of trouble is one of the greatest
ways to bring Him glory. God may allow you to go through difficult times to teach you to call upon Him. By answering your
call, God demonstrates His provision for your life. If God never
allowed you to experience any need, there would be no revela-
tion of your own insufficiency . . . thus, no need to call upon
Him . . . and thus, no opportunity to reveal His sufficiency
(His glory) to others. A life with no troubles can lead to a life of

independence (the opposite of God-dependence), which is the greatest hindrance to a life that glorifies God.

Our times of trouble are times of opportunity that should be expected. To encounter troubles or suffering in this life is not a matter of *if* but *when*. The apostle Peter said, "But rejoice that you participate in the sufferings of Christ, so that you may be overjoyed when his glory is revealed" (1 Pet. 4:13).

Are you going through a trial in your life right now that seems too much to bear? Are you trying to get through it by yourself or by calling upon the One who is waiting to help? To be willing to suffer for the glory of God comes with time and maturity. And the rewards of provision and perseverance become a reflection of His glory in you.

Heavenly Father,

Please give me grace to depend on You, especially in the hard times, so that my life glorifies Your name. Amen.

———— *For the rest of your life . . .* ————

use your trials as a path from independence to God-dependence.

88

When Nothing Is the
Best Thing to Say

*"If only you would be altogether silent!
For you, that would be wisdom."*

JOB 13:5

Often when our friends are hurting, we want to jump right in and save them with just the right words. "It must be God's will," we say, or, "He will work this out for good." We are desperate to "fix" the problem when, in fact, maybe God has allowed the problem for a reason. Instead of removing the problem, God may have a lesson to teach through it. What our friends really need when life does not make sense is not our mouths but our ears.

Job, that faithful man of God who suffered tragically during his life, was also frustrated because his friends wanted to fix his problem with their words. They figured it must be Job's sins that brought on his bad fortune. But Job's friends were not paying attention to what he was really saying. They hardly listened to Job's words. Even worse, they didn't listen to his heart.

Many of us are poor listeners. Children get frustrated because parents want to interrupt with quick answers. Wives get frustrated because husbands want the "bottom line." The best type of support person you can be to your hurting friend is to be a caregiver, not a cure giver" A caregiver shares in the pain, but a cure giver can make it worse. The caregiver cares about the hurting person and his disabilities, but cure givers care more about themselves and their own abilities. The caregiver is a friend who walks with you, whereas cure givers drag you along behind them. Caregivers listen more than they speak, and cure givers speak more than they listen.

There are certain times when words can bring just the right comfort to someone in need, but there are many more times when nothing is the best thing to say.

Ask God to give you a discerning heart. Next time let the one in need lead the way. You may discover that your nonverbal help is far more effective than anything verbal you have to offer.

Heavenly Father,

Help me to be for others the kind of listener You are to me: patient, always available, empathetic, and tenderhearted. May my words to others be those You speak to me. Amen.

--- *For the rest of your life . . .* ---

tell your friends how much you love them,
using words as a last resort.

THE POWER OF PRAISE

I will extol the LORD at all times; his praise
will always be on my lips.

PSALM 34:1

*K*ing David of Israel has to be one of the most unusual
heads of state in history. I like him because he is always
"out there"—not holding anything back, telling us exactly what
he thinks, and praising God with effusiveness and emotion.
When is the last time you heard on the news about a king or
president dancing "with all his might" before the Lord, in front
of his subjects, wearing nothing but the equivalent of today's
T-shirt (a linen ephod; 2 Sam. 6:14)? That's what David did, and
we love him for it.

Today David would probably be a hands-raised, amen-
shouting, sitting-down-front member of the praise and worship
team at his church. Almost everything David wrote (his psalms)
exudes praise in one way or another. David was comfortable with
God; he praised Him for what He had done, was doing now,
and was going to do in the future. And he didn't hesitate to ask
God questions and praise Him for the answers he was confident
would follow.

We were created for the purpose of praise. Paul wrote in the beginning of his letter to the Ephesians, "Praise be to the God and Father of our Lord Jesus Christ. . . . In him we were also chosen . . . in order that we, who were the first to hope in Christ, might be for the praise of his glory" (Eph. 1:3, 11–12). If you are a follower of Christ, it is for the purpose of you bringing praise to God through your life.

What does that mean? It definitely doesn't mean walking around spouting off religious language in order to prove how "born again" you are. Rather it means what it meant for Jesus: to live life at God's initiative, not our own; to obey Him in all things; to serve Him with our lives; to be humbly submissive to His will. Living a life that praises God is the opposite of one that detracts from His glory.

The "joyful noise" (Ps. 100:1 KJV) that we make with our lives is something people will see as much as (probably more than) hear.

Heavenly Father,

I want to be a reflection of Your glory. Please make me aware of anything in my life that takes from instead of adds to Your glory in this world. Amen.

For the rest of your life . . .

find your own way to dance before the Lord with all your might.

OUR HEAVENLY HOME

"And if I go and prepare a place for you, I will come
back and take you to be with me that
you also may be where I am."

JOHN 14:3

As a young girl I always thought one of the best parts of trips or vacations was returning home. Not that I didn't love the changes in scenery and experiences of new places. But there was just something "right" about pulling in the driveway and seeing the old and familiar—those things that temporary places can't provide. I still feel that way today.

Home is all about acceptance, love, and security. It is a place where my needs are met, a place where I can lay down my burdens. All the pressures, responsibilities, and problems of everyday life pale in comparison to the comfort home offers. Even when I fail or fall short, home is a place of forgiveness, restoration, and renewal, and, most of all, love.

Our Father's house is a home in heaven prepared especially for His spiritual children. Jesus told His disciples He was going to prepare a home for them where they would one day join Him (John 14:3). I believe Paul's statement that "no eye has seen, no ear has heard, no mind has conceived what God has prepared for those who love him" (1 Cor. 2:9) must certainly apply to our heavenly home as well as our earthly life in the Spirit.

Our heavenly home will be a place of relief and release from the sufferings and cares of this world (see Rev. 21:3–4). We will be reunited with those who have gone home ahead of us and be introduced to that innumerable cloud of witnesses that has populated heaven for ages (see Heb. 12:1). We will spend all of eternity living in the perfect light of God (see Rev. 21:11; 22:5).

Even today, when I return to the home where I was raised, my aging parents wait to greet me with open arms, and it still feels so right. Likewise God is waiting for you and me to welcome us with open arms to our heavenly home. Like the father of the prodigal son (see Luke 15:11–32), God will never mention our failures when we arrive. He will just want us to know how glad He is to have us home.

Heavenly Father,

Thank You for providing a home in heaven for me through Christ. Thank You that no matter where I have been You always welcome me home. Amen.

———— *For the rest of your life . . .* ————

for the sake of your own family,
make your earthly home as heaven-like as possible.

STUDY QUESTIONS
(NUMBERED TO MATCH THE NUMBERS ON THE DEVOTIONALS)

DEVOTIONAL #1, Prescription for Rest

1. In general, what percent of your life is lived in a condition of spiritual rest? (Minority? Half? Majority?) Explain the reason(s) for your answer.

2. What is your personal "prescription for rest"? How often do you "take" this medicine? How effective is it?

3. How many of God's promises from Scripture have you committed to memory? How does the Holy Spirit use the verses we have memorized?

DEVOTIONAL #2, Why We Worry

1. Faith and fear are both ways of looking at the future. Why can't they coexist? Why is, "I'm trusting God, but I'm still worried" a contradictory statement?

2. About what kinds of issues are you most tempted to worry? For what reason(s) have you decided God is not to be trusted with those matters?

3. Why is biblical contentment not a passive form of resignation? How does one exercise contentment in a proactive way?

DEVOTIONAL #3, A Calm in the Storm

1. Why do you grow more when Jesus calms you instead of the storm? Why does calming you require a deeper level of trust?

2. Where do you find yourself tuning in for guidance most frequently—to Jesus or to the world? Why is guidance that is easiest to obtain often not the most valuable?

3. How have you learned to trust the Lord in the midst of stormy circumstances? What is the promise to which you cling most consistently?

DEVOTIONAL #4, Being before Doing

1. If you had to describe your personality, would you say you are a "doer" or a "be-er"? Do you identify more with Martha or with Mary? Generally speaking, do you focus more on "doing for" or "being with" Jesus?

2. Why is being with Jesus a prerequisite to doing for Jesus? What impact should spending time with Jesus have on what we do?

3. What differences have you observed in the lives of people you know who spend consistent time devotionally with the Lord? What differences have you noted in your life between seasons of spending time versus not spending time with Him?

DEVOTIONAL #5, Digging Your Roots Deeper

1. What is the purpose of God's pruning in your life? Why is pruning so often painful? By definition, is pruning always an uncomfortable process? Why?

2. What is your personal response to the pruning God does in your life? Do you welcome it or resist it? What should your response be? Explain.

3. Who are the people in your life that God uses as "pruners"? How would it help your relationship with them if you began seeing them as tools in God's hands?

DEVOTIONAL #6, Taming the Tongue

1. How would you define *gossip*? When does sharing information cross the line and become gossip?

2. Why is listening to gossip equally as wrong as being the source of gossip? What should you do when someone begins to tell you something inappropriate?

3. Which parts of James 1:19 describe you and which don't? Why is being slow to speak a safeguard against sinning with the tongue?

DEVOTIONAL #7, His Strength in Your Weakness

1. What are some areas of weakness in your life that require you to trust in Christ's strength? Are you glad for those weaknesses, or would you like to be stronger in those areas?

2. What are your strengths? How do you trust Christ in areas where you are naturally strong? What temptation (self-sufficiency) exists when we are strong?

3. If God's goal is to teach us to trust in Him, what can we expect Him to strip us of throughout our Christian life? How receptive are you to His doing that work in you?

DEVOTIONAL #8, Guilt: True or False?

1. What does true guilt feel like to you? How about false guilt? How can you tell the difference between the two?

2. What should happen to the feelings of true guilt when we confess our sins to God and receive His forgiveness? What happens to our guilty feelings when we confess false guilt? Why don't they go away?

3. What should you do if you're not sure of the source of feelings of guilt and shame? How can the Holy Spirit help you if you ask Him?

DEVOTIONAL #9, Growing through Failure

1. What is your response to your own failures—whether it's sin or failure to accomplish a goal? What role does perfectionism

play in your life? What's the difference between perfectionism and excellence?

2. How do you find the balance between God's forgiveness and acceptance and not being satisfied with mediocrity? Why do you continue to pursue success even after failing?

3. How does our culture influence your thoughts about your own failures? How is failure viewed in the Bible compared to the culture? Which is the healthier view?

DEVOTIONAL #10, Healing God's Way

1. What in your life needs healing today? For which of those healings are you actively pursuing God's answer? Would an outside observer conclude you had great faith or little faith regarding God's answer?

2. What balance should there be between consigning yourself to being healed of everything in heaven versus actively seeking healing now? How do you define *contentment* (trust)?

3. What would you tell a friend to do who confided in you about being diagnosed with a terminal illness? How would you encourage her to order her priorities and goals?

DEVOTIONAL #11, The Peace of God

1. What events, circumstances, or facts present the greatest temptation for you to become anxious? To what degree have you developed a pattern, or habitual response, of anxiety concerning

these? Are you becoming more peaceful or more anxious as time progresses?

2. How successful are you at living in a peaceful state? Why is denying reality not the door to peace? Why is acknowledging reality, which includes God's sovereignty, the mature (biblical) route to true peace?

3. Philippians 4:6–7 talks about committing anxious thoughts to God and receiving peace. Is that your pattern the moment you feel anxious? Is prayer for peace an active or passive act? What do you have to do after praying?

DEVOTIONAL #12, The Brevity of Life

1. If you were asked to divide your life into three or four stages or periods, what one-word title would you give to each stage? How do you feel about where you are in life right now?

2. Since hindsight is always perfect, what are the most important spiritual lessons you've learned? What mistakes do you want to avoid? How are your priorities changing?

3. How would you define "living for eternity"? How do you make fixing breakfast for your family an eternal act? Why is it OK with God to occasionally "do nothing"?

DEVOTIONAL #13, A Heart for the Harvest

1. Name as many things as you can that you believe must break the heart of God. How does a Christian go about

developing a heart like that? How do you learn what breaks God's heart?

2. What is your practice when approached by people on the street seeking money or help? If you respond, what do you give them (money? the gospel? advice?)? If you don't respond, what are your reasons?

3. How do you view telephone and mail solicitations from Christian ministries? Do you dismiss them as annoyances or see them as possible opportunities? How does one develop the ability to see everything with God's eyes and act accordingly?

DEVOTIONAL #14, Seeking a Miracle

1. How often do you ask God for a miracle? Do you usually ask for yourself or for others? Is there anything besides need that dictates how often you ask? What are the other factors?

2. What role does faith play in asking God for big things? To what degree do you believe God allows us to have big needs in order to build our faith? Do big needs crush your faith or build your faith? Which should they do?

3. How do you respond if a miracle is not forthcoming? Is your faith in faith or in God? Why is that distinction important?

DEVOTIONAL #15, An Angel of Encouragement

1. Who do you encourage on a regular basis? Does encouragement come naturally for you, or is it something you have to plan? What difference should Christ living in you make?

2. Who encourages you? How do you get encouragement from God when no one else is around? Why is both divine and human encouragement important?

3. Besides words, what tangible or material expressions of encouragement have you shown to another person in the last month? How does the biblical notion of "reap what you sow" determine how much encouragement you receive?

DEVOTIONAL #16, Hearing the Silence of God

1. What is your typical reaction when you pray and seem not to hear a reply from God? Keep praying? Give up? Get frustrated or angry? What do you think your response should be?

2. We see events as they happen whereas God sees everything at once—past, present, and future. How should that make a difference when we don't immediately hear a response from God to our prayers? How might it help you to be more patient?

3. In what sense is God's silence an answer? What does His silence say? What other answers to our prayers are there besides "yes" and "no"?

DEVOTIONAL #17, Discovering Who You Are

1. What is the difference between who you really are, who others think you are, and who you think you are? Which of those forms the largest part of your image of yourself?

2. To what degree is your life—your behavior and expectations—consistent with who you think you are? Which

do you try to correct most often—your self-image or your behavior? Which should take priority?

3. Why is the Bible the best place to look for an accurate picture of who you are? What will you find about yourself in the Bible that you won't find anywhere else? When you find your self-perception varying from what the Bible says ("I am not a valuable person."), what should you do?

DEVOTIONAL #18, A Godly Heritage

1. Compare what you "caught" from, and were taught by, your parents. Which has had the most lasting impact? How has your spiritual life been helped or hindered by the environment in which you grew up?

2. If you are a parent, are you focusing more on teaching your children or trying to show them Jesus in your life? Is one of these more important than the other? How quick are you to ask forgiveness of your children when your example isn't what it should be?

3. What do you believe is the most important thing you can teach your children? How are you trying to accomplish that priority? What would you most like for your children to remember about you when you're gone?

DEVOTIONAL #19, The Call to Obedience

1. Why is obedience, regardless of the realm (parenting, marriage, or relating to God), an evidence of love?

2. What are some possible motives people might have for obeying God? What is the only valid motive?

3. In what area(s) of life is obedience to Christ a challenge for you? Why is "will" more important than "feelings" when it comes to obedience?

DEVOTIONAL #20, Our Refuge from Fear

1. What are your top three fears in life? How many of them are issues you have control over? How much sense does it make to live in fear of that which is beyond your reach?

2. How many of your fears are "inherited"—fears you picked up in the environment in which you were raised or from others? How should being a "new creation" in Christ impact your former fears? In the environment of God's kingdom, how out of place is fear?

3. Both faith and fear address the future. Why is faith in a sovereign God better than fear when it comes to the future? Which can actually impact how the future turns out?

DEVOTIONAL #21, The Cure of Loneliness

1. What is the difference between being alone and being lonely? What makes one painful and the other not?

2. What are the warning signs of loneliness? What should you do when you notice these signs?

3. Practically speaking, how can Christ's presence overcome loneliness?

DEVOTIONAL #22, The Perfect Parent

1. What have you come to know and appreciate most about your heavenly Father's "parenting style"? What does He do toward you that you would like to do toward your own children?

2. A steward is a manager of another's property. How does being a steward (instead of an owner) of the children God has entrusted to you change your idea of parenting? How does it change the "I'm not in this alone" factor?

3. How has God used the challenges of parenthood to change your life? How does that make parenting as much about you as about your children?

DEVOTIONAL #23, Witnessing without Words

1. How did you feel about people witnessing to you before you became a Christian? How has that experience helped you be more sensitive to how you share the gospel now?

2. If a friend asked you today to help her become a Christian, would you know how? What are the fundamental, "nonnegotiables" of the gospel of Jesus Christ?

3. What are the advantages of spreading the gospel "without words"? What are the dangers (e.g., never getting around to explaining the gospel)? What role can fear of offending play in relying too much on "witnessing without words"?

DEVOTIONAL #24, Am I Good Enough?

1. How does the competitive nature of our culture force us to compare ourselves with others? What is the inevitable result of such comparisons on one's self-image?

2. How does the Bible's statement, "For all have sinned," put everyone on the same plane in God's sight? How does that make God's grace all the more important as a means of acceptance with Him?

3. How does being accepted by grace by God encourage you to accept others on the same basis? How does it help you to know that no one is too good to be loved by you or too bad not to be loved by you?

DEVOTIONAL #25, Taking Up the Cross

1. If a Christian never suffers from "spiritual exhaustion," what might that be a sign of? In what capacities are you serving Christ that are a challenge? What motivation do you use to continue?

2. What are some examples of carnal motivations to serve Christ? What are examples of spiritual motivations? What tempts you to serve for the wrong reasons, and how do you combat those temptations?

3. Explain in your words, accurately and graphically, what Christ did for you at Calvary? How would a "devalued" version be different? Why is our service for Christ a good indicator of how we view what He did for us?

STUDY QUESTIONS

DEVOTIONAL #26, Facts First, Then Feelings

1. What consistent efforts do you make to increase your knowledge of the facts (truth) of Christianity? As you have grown in knowledge, have you noticed a difference in the emotional ups and downs in your life? Why should you have?

2. What negative emotions (anger, fear, jealousy, etc.) are you most prone to experiencing? How can truth (the Bible) help you overcome these feelings? What strategy could you use to specifically target these areas of weakness?

3. Why should you not try to suppress positive emotions such as joy and excitement? Why are some "down" emotions like grief and sorrow healthy? What is the key to staying emotionally balanced?

DEVOTIONAL #27, Depressed but Not Destroyed

1. What is the difference between suffering with no hope and suffering with hope? What is the difference between "hope" and hope that is grounded in biblical truth?

2. Even if you are a Christian, how might your response to suffering fail to reveal the life of Christ in you? What was Christ's response to His suffering? If He lives in you, how should response to your suffering be a reflection of His response?

3. Why is suffering, even death, not the "end of the road" for a Christian? Why does the world look at Christians as "crazy people" when they see us living with hope? How is suffering a form of evangelism?

STUDY QUESTIONS

DEVOTIONAL #28, The Purpose of Prayer

1. Describe how your prayer life has changed as a Christian. For what kinds of "things" do you mostly pray?

2. How often do you experience the pleasure of God's presence in prayer? Should you expect to experience that pleasure consistently?

3. How have you found that prayer changes you?

DEVOTIONAL #29, Living above the Circumstances

1. What set of circumstances is most likely to put you in the valley of despair? How could you prepare ahead of time for those circumstances?

2. When you are on a mountain peak of excitement, what is the only direction you can go? Why is living on an even plane more emotionally profitable in the long run?

3. Why is it better to focus on God changing you than changing your circumstances? If you stay close to Jesus, how will you relate to the circumstances in your life?

DEVOTIONAL #30, Knowing God Personally

1. What person do you know best in this world? Why do you know this person better than all others? How many of those same factors are true of your relationship with Christ?

2. What extra effort is required to get to know a person who is not present physically? List the best ways you can think of to

get to know Christ deeply and personally and how effective you are in pursuing those ways.

3. What traits do you first notice in a person who knows Christ well? Over time, what other traits surface in his or her life? How does that person's life impact you as an example or motivation?

DEVOTIONAL #31, Your Body, His Temple

1. On a scale of one to ten (ten being "great"), how would you rate your stewardship of your body? Has treating your body as God's temple been a prime motivator, or have you had other reasons for trying to stay fit?

2. What are the primary obstacles to keeping yourself healthy and fit? Does viewing fitness as a matter of stewardship give you any fresh incentive? Why or why not?

3. Considering the whole person as God's temple, how do you maintain emotional fitness? Spiritual fitness? If you were dwelling inside a person just like you, how would you rate the experience?

DEVOTIONAL #32, Divine Love

1. What part do your feelings play in your perception of whether God loves you (is pleased with you as His child)? What would help you begin separating your feelings from the fact of His love? (Scripture memory? Self-talk?)

2. Do you see parallels between your ability to receive God's love and the way your parents loved you? Why should the fact of your being "born again" give you a fresh perspective on your new "heavenly parent" (God the Father)?

3. What connection have you found between your own feelings of "unlovability" and the way you love others (spouse, children, coworkers)? How could you use your actions toward others as a reminder that you are loved unconditionally by God?

DEVOTIONAL #33, Setting Priorities

1. What or who is the highest priority in your life? If five people who know you well were asked to name your highest priority, what would they say?

2. As a Christian, if God is your highest priority, how does your life reflect that commitment? Other than activities (quiet time, church, etc.) how do you make Christ and His values your top priority?

3. What is the difference between Christianity and Christ as a top priority in life? Why is it easier to make Christianity a higher priority than Christ?

DEVOTIONAL #34, Blessings of Brokenness

1. Based on your reading of this devotional, define in your own words "the blessing of brokenness." Why is brokenness a blessing we don't have to seek on our own?

2. How has difficulty in your life changed since becoming a Christian? Is life easier or harder? In what ways? What has surprised you, if anything, about difficulties since coming to know Christ?

3. Compare the effect difficulties had on your life as a non-Christian with their effect in your life as a Christian. How has being a Christian changed the way you view difficulties?

Devotional #35, A Marriage Made in Heaven

1. Why do so many people experience disappointment in their marriage? What is the connection between expectations and disappointment? What is the connection between assumed rights and expectations?

2. How can focusing on *doing* right instead of *being* right completely change one's expectations about the performance of another person? What constitutes "doing right" in a marriage?

3. Why does service result in more change than confrontation and demands for change? How does serving Christ in one's life naturally lead to serving one's spouse?

Devotional #36, A Childlike Faith

1. How would your life be different if you woke up every morning like a trusting, confident, child? To what degree do you anticipate all your needs being met at the beginning of each day?

2. How does one find the balance between adult responsibilities and childlike faith? How does a mature adult maintain a childlike nature in the midst of planning, scheduling, working, and otherwise being "responsible"?

3. Give some examples of those things God holds you responsible for and those things He doesn't. How can keeping these two lists separate help you maintain a childlike trust in God?

DEVOTIONAL #37, The Battle of the Mind

1. How much of what you "worshipped" as a non-Christian is still a part of your life as a Christian? Is it there by choice? What keeps you from tearing down "the high places"?

2. If someone who didn't know you studied your checkbook and your calendar, what would they conclude about what you "worship"? Why are our time and money good indicators of that which is most important to us?

3. What efforts do you make to renew your mind by focusing on godly things? What do you include in and exclude from your life? How much time do you spend meditating on and memorizing the Word of God?

DEVOTIONAL #38, Losing Your Life

1. What experiences have you had that validate the paradoxes in the kingdom of God (giving to receive, dying to live, etc.)? What faith commitment is required up front to live this

way—stepping out in obedience before seeing results? How challenging is this for you?

2. Compare your "before Christ" and "since Christ" experiences of finding yourself. To what degree have you found yourself since "losing yourself" in Christ? What have you gained as a result of losing yourself in Christ?

3. How would you explain the concept of "losing yourself to find yourself" to a non-Christian or new Christian? How do you personally die to yourself in an ongoing way as a Christian?

DEVOTIONAL #39, The Service of the Saintly

1. Can you recall a time when you performed an act of service that you felt was behind the scenes, even inconsequential, which God used in an unexpected way? What did you learn from the experience?

2. Why should service be undertaken regardless of expected or unexpected results? Why is service by itself a worthy pursuit? How does the server benefit?

3. How do pride and humility affect our willingness to serve? When we feel a task is beneath us, what kind of warning should that set off?

DEVOTIONAL #40, Making Decisions

1. What "good" does God accomplish through the things that happen in our lives? (see Rom. 8:28) What measure of

freedom, instead of fear, does that provide for us to walk in faith into the future?

2. What keeps you from making decisions? Why is predicting the future and all possible variables a fruitless process? How do you integrate your faith into your decision-making processes?

3. How can fear of failure and fear of the future cause us to freeze when it comes to making decisions? How does fear of the results of our decisions show a lack of faith in a sovereign God?

DEVOTIONAL #41, Faith That Acts

1. If you were counseling Peter after his denial of Jesus, what would you have told him? Are there times when you feel like "taking a day off" from your faith? What do you do when you feel that way?

2. Describe a time when you denied (or hid, or fudged, or almost denied) your relationship to Christ. What produced the pressure? How did you recover?

3. What does Jesus seeking out Peter mean to you? What does it say about Jesus' love for us in spite of our failures?

DEVOTIONAL #42, The Purpose of a Fruitful Life

1. What is/are your spiritual gift(s)? How do you know? Where are you using your gifts in the body of Christ?

2. Do you think Paul's list of nine spiritual fruits in Galatians 5:22–23 is complete? Are there more than nine dimensions to

Jesus' personality? What other evidences of Jesus' life are there that the Spirit might manifest through you?

3. Have you ever tried to minister with your spiritual gift apart from a context of love? What was the result? Why is love the quality that causes spiritual gifts to bear fruit?

DEVOTIONAL #43, When God Calls

1. What dream (big thing) have you nurtured in your heart for years that you would love for God to help you accomplish? Do you believe this is your idea or God's? If you thought it was God's, would you move ahead?

2. Why do people have a hard time believing God would want them to accomplish their dream, that He would call them to do something that makes them happy? How consistent is that with God's role as a Father to His children?

3. How willing are you to do small things for God to see where they might lead? What could you do today to put your dream in motion, to explore partnering with God?

DEVOTIONAL #44, Reaping What We Sow

1. From whom does everything you have come—whether time, talent, or treasure? As a steward (manager) of what you have been given, whom should you consult before using any of it? How consistently do you do that?

2. Do you have a predetermined plan for financial giving, or do you decide at the moment how much to give? From God's

perspective, how does your having a plan enable Him to know how much of a blessing you can be to others as He gives to you?

3. Do you give out of your excess or out of what you sometimes need to live on? Which requires more faith? How does the biblical principle "you reap what you sow" encourage you to be generous?

DEVOTIONAL #45, Unworthy to Serve

1. List all the reasons you can think of for why you are not qualified to serve God. Now list all the people who you think *are* qualified (are holy enough) to serve Him. If perfection was a qualification, who would be able to serve God at all?

2. Why does being born again and having the Holy Spirit living within make you qualified in God's sight? Why did God give you a spiritual gift? How does the idea of the "body of Christ" presuppose that all Christians are called to serve?

3. How quickly does your hand go up when a need is announced? What is more important to God, your skills or your willing spirit?

DEVOTIONAL #46, Living Sacrifices

1. How much of your life have you given over to God? That is, is there any part of your life that you would be unhappy if God asked for it?

2. How much parallel should there be between saying everything is God's and actually, literally giving it to Him? In practical terms, how are we to express the sacrifice of our life to God?

3. If Christ has already sacrificed Himself for us, why does God ask us to sacrifice ourselves as well? Is this a different kind of sacrifice? Different in what way?

DEVOTIONAL #47, The Portrait of a Faithful Woman

1. If God made it clear to you that He had a difficult and dangerous assignment for one of your children, how do you think you would respond? What would be the value in saying "no"? What blessing would come from saying "yes"?

2. Why are difficult assignments from God necessary to build faith? How much is our faith stretched when God asks us to do something easy?

3. Why is, "Your word is my command," a biblical response to live by in the Christian life? How have you let God know there is nothing that is "off the table" when it comes to obeying Him? Is that something you should tell Him today?

DEVOTIONAL #48, Being Born Again

1. Have you been born again? How do you know? Using human growth as an analogy, what stage of spiritual growth are you in now? (Infant? Child? Adolescent? etc.) What are the spiritual marks of that age?

2. The Bible says we become a new creation in Christ when we are born again. What parts of your old life were you happy to leave behind? What are you most enjoying about your new life in Christ?

3. What have you seen in the kingdom of God that you prefer over the kingdom of this world? What has surprised you the most about the kingdom of God? How have your attitudes about Christianity changed since being born again?

DEVOTIONAL #49, God's Will for Your Life

1. How would you define God's will for your life in general terms (the same for every believer) and specifically (what you believe His will is for you personally)? How faithful are you at carrying out God's will that He desires for every believer?

2. Why is carrying out God's *general* will the best way to discover His *specific* will for you? How far into the future do you want to know God's will? How far into the future should you be content with knowing?

3. How much do you worry about not knowing "God's will" for your life? What would you expect a loving Father to do if there was something His children needed? How much time have you spent listening for His direction concerning your future?

DEVOTIONAL #50, Split Personality

1. In what area of life does your "split personality" show itself most readily? What has been your strategy to gain victory?

2. If you are "more than a conqueror" in Christ, why does your old self continue to pose a problem? What is the biblical reason for man's "split personality"? What is the biblical solution?

3. When you get a glimpse of your flesh (your natural self), for what part of your relationship with Christ do you become most thankful? In light of the reality of spiritual struggles, are you ever tempted to "go back"? Why is struggling with Christ better than struggling without Him?

DEVOTIONAL #51, The Perfect Mate

1. How would you define a "perfect mate"? Should your definition have more to do with that person's attributes or the certainty you feel about God's guidance in leading you to that person?

2. Why are there no perfect mates or perfect unions? What, then, should imperfect people do to bring fruit out of imperfection in marriage? What does marriage offer that makes dying to self worth it? List the five most important reasons you want to find a mate.

3. What is the balance between finding a mate and trusting God to bring you a mate? How do you know when you're doing your part versus more than your part? How will you know when the right person arrives?

DEVOTIONAL #52, Traveling Light

1. What kind of baggage—guilt, regret, shame, disappointment—have you brought from your past into your relationship with Christ? What effect(s) does carrying that baggage around have on you?

2. What efforts have you made to get free of these burdens? Are you waiting for God to remove them, or is it more your responsibility to live in the freedom Christ has provided?

3. Even if you are free of burdens and baggage from your past, how often do present burdens like worry and anxiety and fear weigh you down? Why is there no reason for a Christian to be burdened about anything?

DEVOTIONAL #53, Forgiving and Forgiven

1. Is there anyone in your life you have not forgiven? What are the consequences of disobeying God's command to forgive? Which would be worse, to forgive another or to live without God's blessing because of disobedience?

2. Why do we not forgive readily and easily? What twist of logic do we use to justify maintaining a grudge? Why can't we remember from one incident to the next that forgiveness is always better?

3. What price do we pay when we forgive another? What price did God pay when He forgave your sins? What infinite resource does God supply by which you are able to forgive an infinite number of times?

Devotional #54, Never Meet a Stranger

1. In your world who might be the equivalent of a Samaritan, or Samaritan woman, in Jesus' day? How comfortable are you in showing love to them?

2. What is intrinsic to all human beings that makes them worthy of being loved? Whom do we ultimately devalue when we fail to love another person?

3. When you are not loved by someone, how can you use that as a motivation to love in return? What is the difference between loving "because of" and "in spite of"?

Devotional #55, The Divine Coach

1. Why are we willing to accept good things as part of God's plan but not bad things? How hard is it for you to accept difficulties as coming from God?

2. What is your first response when you experience trouble in life? As a Christian, what should your first response be? Should your reaction to life's events be consistently the same, regardless of their nature?

3. Why isn't Romans 8:28 a license "to do whatever we want," knowing God will "fix it" in the end? What does the phrase "those who love Him" suggest about our responsibility in our actions and choices?

DEVOTIONAL #56, Giants in Your Land

1. What are the three largest giants looming on your horizon at present? Can you think of a promise of God by which each can be defeated?

2. Why is the character of the one making the promise so important? In God's case why are His promises trustworthy?

3. What is your responsibility in defeating spiritual giants? Using financial worries as an example, how would you defeat this giant on a day-to-day basis?

DEVOTIONAL #57, Hope When Life Looks Hopeless

1. Explain the difference between the kind of "hoping" we do daily and biblical hope. Why is biblical hope not dependent on the circumstances of the day? On what is it based?

2. Why is hope almost a synonym for faith? Why is "confidence" a good synonym for both? If you are a Christian who lives in hope, what should you be confident about, both temporally and eternally?

3. Why should a Christian have hope? What is the historical (time and space) foundation for hope? Why is biblical hope not the same as "having a good feeling" about something?

DEVOTIONAL #58, A Hunger for Humility

1. Recognizing that pride will make you resist this question, how does pride manifest itself in your life? What pretenses are

you most tempted to maintain? What are you most hesitant to reveal?

2. Why does pride come naturally when humility requires development? Why is humility sometimes painful to exercise (for example, when we have to admit failures)? But why is humility also an evidence of maturity?

3. As you have grown as a Christian, to what degree have you become more willing to expose your failures and weaknesses? Why should you be? Why is it better to humble oneself rather than have God do it?

DEVOTIONAL #59, Using Your Gifts

1. What spiritual gift(s) has God given you? How do you know? How long have you known? How are you using your gift(s)?

2. Why is it important not to confuse natural talents with spiritual gifts? On the other hand, how might they overlap? Why is feedback from others important in determining your spiritual gift(s)?

3. What does it mean to build up the body of Christ? How does your spiritual gift achieve that goal? How is Christ's church affected if you are not exercising your gift(s)?

DEVOTIONAL #60, How's Your Hearing?

1. To what degree do you believe God wants to speak to you? Do you see Him as distant and noncommunicative or close

and talkative? What is the source of these different impressions about God?

2. How do you best hear from God? How do you confirm what you believe God has said to you? What would be the best way to confirm what you hear?

3. How do you view circumstances in your life? As they occur, are you in continual dialogue with God about them—about their meaning? How does God differ from your best friend with whom you would share everything that happens and what you think it means?

DEVOTIONAL #61, Walking through the Valley

1. What do you fear most, if anything, about your own mortality? Regardless of your current age, how are you preparing to die?

2. How have you handled the death of friends or loved ones who are not believers in Christ? What sense of urgency do those deaths create in you about sharing the gospel?

3. What is the difference between fearing death and having a healthy respect for it? Knowing death could arrive at any moment, how does knowing Christ ease your fear?

DEVOTIONAL #62, Spiritual Warfare

1. How conscious are you of the reality of spiritual warfare as you go about your daily life? How often do you connect a

negative event with Satan's interference? Why is forewarned forearmed when it comes to spiritual battle?

2. Why are subtle deceptions and counterfeits more dangerous than outright spiritual attacks? Why is focusing on Christ, not Satan, the best defense against counterfeits?

3. How well versed are you in the believer's spiritual armor? (Eph. 6) How can armor defend you that has not been put on? How should you daily go through the process of putting on your spiritual armor?

DEVOTIONAL #63, The Hurried Christian

1. Concerning what aspects of life are you most impatient? What do you think your impatience reveals about your view of God's sovereignty over all the affairs of life?

2. How would you counsel a younger Christian on what it means to "wait on the Lord"? Specifically, how does one practice the discipline of waiting on God?

3. To what degree does our culture work against the spiritual discipline of patience? What can you do personally to counter that influence?

DEVOTIONAL #64, Creating a New You

1. What kind(s) of marble has God been chipping off of your humanity in order to allow Christ to be revealed? Has it been sudden? Gradual? Painful? How compliant have you been in the process?

2. How does knowing the goal, your Christlikeness—make the process easier? In what ways is Christ becoming more recognizable in you? What aspects of your humanity still overshadow His presence?

3. What have you learned as a Christian about the power of the flesh to resist the work of God? What connection is there between your resistance to God and the pain of His work? How could you lessen the pain?

DEVOTIONAL #65, What Real Faith Looks Like

1. Why is a life-threatening illness (or other situation) a win-win for a Christian? Why is this not a version of "fatalism"? In what historical reality is this optimism grounded?

2. In what kinds of situations in life should the Christian say "not my will but Yours be done"? Why is it harder to say it in the little things than in a big situation where we seemingly have no choice? To what degree should that always be the Christian's response?

3. What guarantees does this world suggest you have a right to? What is the only guarantee that God gives you in Christ? Since you have no guarantee to long life, why does it make sense to yield to God's will every day?

DEVOTIONAL #66, The Goal of Perfection

1. In what areas of your life do you find the healthy pursuit of excellence turning into a carnal (offensive) form of perfectionism? What pushes you over that line?

2. How do you maintain a balance between *being* and *doing* for Christ? In what kinds of circumstances might some other goal be a higher priority than being perfect?

3. When is perfectionism a godly quality, and when does it become carnal? In what areas of your life do you strive for perfectionism? How do you know when you have pushed too hard?

DEVOTIONAL #67, Rising above Rejection

1. What kind(s) of rejection do you fear most? What is at the root of your fear? To what ill-advised lengths have you gone to keep from being rejected?

2. Why does being accepted by God mean not having to fear the rejection of man? To what degree are you willing to be rejected just as Christ was?

3. What forms the basis for being accepted in the eyes of today's culture? What forms the basis for being accepted in the eyes of God?

DEVOTIONAL #68, True Joy

1. How would you define *joy* (and its source)? How is joy different from happiness? Which do you think characterizes your life most often?

2. Since joy is part of the fruit of the Spirit, how is it produced? Do we have a part to play, or is joy all the Spirit's work?

3. In what kinds of situations is joy most needed? Is happiness any less valuable? How does each contribute to presenting a balanced life to non-Christians?

DEVOTIONAL #69, Letting Go

1. With what aspect of your future do you have the most consistent "faith versus fear" struggle? What part of that area do you feel God is incapable of handling?

2. How would you feel if Jesus Christ personally (physically) accompanied you through your day? Would you ever have reason to fear? Why does the presence of the Holy Spirit not give you the same comfort?

3. Why didn't God promise, "your life will be easy," instead of promising, "I'll never leave you"? Why is the latter the better promise? Why does God want us to go through challenging times?

DEVOTIONAL #70, Filled with the Spirit

1. How does a Christian become filled with the Spirit? If you had to explain this concept to a new Christian, what would you say?

2. How do you know you are filled with the Spirit? What role does faith play? What can result in your not being filled with the Spirit?

3. What impact should being filled with the Spirit have on daily affairs such as decisions and responding to unforeseen

challenges? Explain how you can be filled with the Spirit and still, in retrospect, realize you could have made a better decision. How does being filled with the Spirit intersect with spiritual or emotional maturity?

DEVOTIONAL #71, Patience through Suffering

1. What difference does it make that James 1:2 says "when," not "if," you have trials? Are you surprised by life's difficulties or have you learned to accept them as normal?

2. What would Satan like you to believe about God during a difficult period of trouble? Why is God glorified when we maintain our trust in Him during hard times? Why does God's name suffer when we fail to trust Him?

3. Explain what it means to see all of life from God's perspective? What does God see that you can't? How could you learn to gain God's perspective on life?

DEVOTIONAL #72, Waiting on God

1. If you prayed, "Lord, please prioritize my day," how would He do that? What is your responsibility in the day after praying that prayer?

2. Why do we view people who say "no" as uncaring—but not view Jesus that way? Why was He willing to say "no" when we aren't?

3. How consistently do you spend time waiting on God in prayer to receive direction for your life? What difference would it make if you increased that time?

DEVOTIONAL #73, Financial Security

1. How do you prove to yourself on a consistent basis that money is not your source of security? To what degree is your mood—contentedness, worry, peace, anxiety—tied to your finances?

2. For you (and/or your family), how much money is enough? What are your financial goals? How does giving factor into your personal financial goals?

3. Do you plan to elevate your lifestyle as your income or resources increase? Is that necessary? How does a Christian acquire the ability to begin doing other things with money besides spending it on self?

DEVOTIONAL #74, The Crown of Perseverance

1. How do trials affect your spiritual life? Do they cause your roots to sink deeper into Christ or cause you to seek relief elsewhere?

2. Are you able to maintain a time of daily devotions with the Lord in spite of distractions? What things have become more pressing than spending a few minutes alone with God? How might your distractions decrease if you took time to pray about them?

3. Since becoming a Christian, how has your perseverance (your commitment) increased or decreased? To what do you owe your progress or regress? Are you shaping the world, or is the world shaping you?

DEVOTIONAL #75, Complete Surrender

1. How do you respond to the biblical notion of being a loser at life—of being unable to "fix" your relationship with God on your own? Why did Jesus say you couldn't be His disciple without letting go of even yourself?

2. What evidence do you see in the world at large that man has been unsuccessful at creating a sustainable world on *his* own? What evidence do you see in your life that, apart from Christ, your world would be just as chaotic?

3. What does the Bible promise to those who surrender all to Christ? Why is it harder to surrender all than to make it on one's own? Why is it also better in the long run?

DEVOTIONAL #76, Who Do You Think You Are?

1. How much of your self-perception is a result of what you've been told by others? Have you been told that you're "OK" or "not OK"? How does your perceived success in life match what you believe about yourself?

2. Who do you believe knows better than all others what you should know about yourself? What efforts do you make to take in His opinions about you above all others?

3. How have you seen God's truth about you change your self-perception, and thus your life? Why is Paul's exhortation to "renew your mind" (see Rom. 12:2) a key to knowing who you really are?

DEVOTIONAL #77, Believe It or Not

1. What is the difference between having faith in faith and faith in God through Jesus Christ? Why is the object of our faith the most important element of all? Of what use is faith in an impotent object?

2. What should you do to increase your faith in God? If you never exercise your faith, how strong will it ever become?

3. What issues in your life are currently problematic or unresolved? How diligently have you exercised faith in prayer concerning them? Based on Jesus' words, what might happen if your faith was stronger?

DEVOTIONAL #78, Transformed by Truth

1. Over recent weeks, how many times have you "failed a pop quiz"—been anxious, angry, despairing, fudged the truth, etc? What does that tell you about your preparedness for life's tests?

2. In a perfect world how would you prepare daily before going out into the world? Of what would your spiritual preparation consist? What kind of daily preparation (quiet time) do you make now? How could you close the gap between the two?

3. How does God use information to bring about transformation? Why is just reading the Bible not enough? What else is necessary?

DEVOTIONAL #79, Principles of Prayer

1. Think of people that you approach in certain ways when you want to talk (spouse, boss, child). Why do you do that? Is it being manipulative or being wise?

2. How do you establish the balance between being personal and intimate with God yet respecting His majesty and holiness? How has modern culture diminished the practice of respecting those who are in places of authority?

3. How would you define "the fear of the Lord"? As true fear? As respect and awe? As both? Should we be afraid of God in any way?

DEVOTIONAL #80, The Treasure of Your Heart

1. Why do you think Jesus said that your heart will follow your treasure instead of your treasure following your heart? Where does that put the priority in terms of what you do with your time, talent, and treasure?

2. Understanding that much of life is devoted to fulfilling obligations like work and family, what does your life reveal about what you treasure when you have a chance to choose? How closely do your choices match your confessions—your walk match your talk?

3. How do you "self-examine," continually assess your commitments and behaviors? Small group? Spousal interaction? Prayer? If you are not "self-examining," how do you know you are living like you think you are?

DEVOTIONAL #81, Nourishing Your Soul

1. What symptoms do you notice when you become spiritually malnourished? How often do you seek to ease the symptoms with spiritual "junk food" instead of spending time with God?

2. When you have free time—even a few minutes—how do you choose to spend it? How often do you stop to pray, to meditate on Scripture memory cards, or read your Bible or another edifying Christian book? What do your choices say to you?

3. Compare your regularity in consuming God's Word with your regularity in consuming food. In which are you most consistent? Why are most people more disciplined about eating than spending time with God?

DEVOTIONAL #82, Secret of Submission

1. List all the people to whom you have to submit, regularly or occasionally, in your life. What is God showing you about yourself in the situations where submitting is not easy?

2. Why do you think there is more honor and strength in submitting than in dominating? (Why does it take more grace to be humble than to be proud?) Why is submitting an effective way to win an opponent?

3. To whom did Christ submit in His life (and even in death)? What do you learn about submission from observing His willingness to humble himself before others?

DEVOTIONAL #83, Being Still

1. Who is ultimately responsible for your daily schedule, for making time to spend alone with the Lord?

2. What is the difference between being still physically and being still spiritually? Can you be still spiritually in the midst of a hectic day?

3. What should you do when you call out to God but hear no immediate answer?

DEVOTIONAL #84, God Wants All Your Concerns

1. What is the smallest level of concern with which you feel comfortable "bothering" God? Where did you get the idea that there are some things too small for His attention?

2. What about matters that are embarrassing for you to bring up, especially sins and failures that you've confessed many times before? Does God ever reach the end of His patience? How does His patience differ from ours?

3. How comfortable are you with biblical exhortations to be shameless, bold, and confident when entering God's presence? Do you think God appreciates His children coming with confidence? Why or why not?

DEVOTIONAL #85, Believing God

1. Explain in your own words the difference between "believing in God" and "believing God." Have you done the former? How well do you do the latter?

2. What are you believing God for right now? (What are you sure of that you do not currently see?)

3. Why is it dangerous to live the Christian life by sight instead of by faith? How do you find a balance between the reality you see (walking by sight) and the reality you hope to see (walking by faith)? How do you explain it when faith has to yield to reality?

DEVOTIONAL #86, Confession Counts

1. How big a part of your life is confession of sin to God? Are you in the habit of confessing sins immediately? What is the danger if you don't?

2. How hard is it for you to confess a sin you've committed against another person and to humbly ask his or her forgiveness? If you can ask God's forgiveness but not the person against whom you sinned, what does that say?

3. What eventually happens to the heart of a person who doesn't confess his sins? Why does the embarrassment and shame of confession make us less likely to sin as easily?

DEVOTIONAL #87, Glorifying God

1. How often do you refer to God as your source of strength when talking with others—especially with non-Christians? How much is God glorified when we don't give Him credit in our lives?

2. How do troubles in life force you to call upon God? How does choosing God over all other "gods" bring glory to Him? How is He not glorified above all others by your not choosing Him? How do you make your choice known?

3. What are you going through right now that could serve as a catalyst for glorifying God? How did Christ's suffering glorify God? How can yours if you call on Him? How does God's glory add a new dimension to our suffering in this life?

DEVOTIONAL #88, When Nothing Is the Best Thing to Say

1. How hard is it for you not to dispense advice and solutions to a person who is hurting? Why is listening and refraining from advice a greater challenge than talking? Why are most people uncomfortable with silence?

2. What does God seem to do most when we talk to Him in prayer? Whose voice is allowed to take the lead in the conversation? Why is this a good model to use in our care-giving efforts?

3. From your reading of the Bible and your own spiritual experience, is God more interested in fixing problems or teaching us through the problem? What is the tendency in our culture? How much are Christians influenced by the fix-it mentality?

DEVOTIONAL #89, The Power of Praise

1. What does it mean to you to know you were chosen "for the praise of his glory"? How consistently does your life fulfill that purpose? What aspects of your life detract from that purpose?

2. How often do you hide your relationship with Christ from the world? How is that attitude contrary to living a life "for the praise of his glory"? Whose commendation would you rather have, God's or the world's? What keeps you from identifying with Christ at every opportunity?

3. How can you best praise God nonverbally? Which is more powerful—verbal or nonverbal praise? With which are you most comfortable? How can nonverbal praise lead to an opportunity to make it verbal?

DEVOTIONAL #90, Our Heavenly Home

1. How do you picture heaven in terms of "home"? How much do you anticipate arriving there? If you had the option, would you proceed immediately to heaven or would you be hesitant to leave earth? In either case, why?

2. What characteristics of heaven might you be able to build into your own home as a reflection of "heaven on earth"? To what degree are people attracted to your home because of the presence of God in it? To what degree should they be?

3. As a heavenly Father, what do you most appreciate about God as the head of your spiritual home? How do you emulate those same characteristics toward your own children to whet their appetite for God?

Scripture Index

Subject Index